AI agents for beginners:

A practice-oriented introduction

Imprint

Information according to Section 5 of the E-Commerce Act (ECG) and Section 14 of the Austrian Commercial Code (UGB):

Author and editor
Gerald Oswald, MBA
Krappgasse 5
A- 3712 Maissau
Austria

Contact
email: imprint@oswald.energy

Responsible for the content according to § 55 para. 2 RStV
Gerald Oswald, Krappgasse 5, A-3712 Maissau, Austria

ISBN : 9798280280267

Table of contents

Part I: Introduction to AI and Agents

- **Chapter 1:** What is Artificial Intelligence? Introduction and Basic Concepts
- **Chapter 2:** Intelligent Agents: Definition and Examples
- **Chapter 3:** History of AI and the Development of Agents
- **Chapter 4:** AI agents in everyday life: current applications

Part II: Theoretical Foundations of AI Agents

- **Chapter 5:** Fundamentals of Intelligent Agents: Perception, Actions and Environment
- **Chapter 6:** Types of AI agents: reflexive, goal-oriented and utility-based agents
- **Chapter 7:** Learning Agents: Introduction to Machine Learning
- **Chapter 8:** Problem Solving Through Search: Basic Search Algorithms
- **Chapter 9:** Heuristic Search and Optimization Methods
- **Chapter 10:** Knowledge-Based Agents and Knowledge Representation
- **Chapter 11:** Inference Mechanisms and Logical Reasoning
- **Chapter 12:** Planning and Decision Making for Agents
- **Chapter 13:** Dealing with Uncertainty: Probabilistic Approaches
- **Chapter 14:** Reinforcement Learning: Reward-Based Learning
- **Chapter 15:** Multi-Agent Systems: Fundamentals and Concepts
- **Chapter 16:** Communication and Cooperation between Agents

Part III: Practical Development of AI Agents

- **Chapter 17:** Approach to developing AI agents
- **Chapter 18:** Defining Requirements and Setting Goals
- **Chapter 19:** Modeling and Design of the Agent
- **Chapter 20:** Selection of suitable algorithms and data structures
- **Chapter 21:** Implementation: Programming a Simple Agent
- **Chapter 22:** Testing and Validating Agent Behavior
- **Chapter 23:** Training and Learning: Developing a Learning Agent
- **Chapter 24:** Optimizing and Improving Agent Performance
- **Chapter 25:** Case Study: Developing a Complete AI Agent

Part IV: Technical Tools and Frameworks

- **Chapter 26:** Programming languages and development environments for AI agents
- **Chapter 27:** Important Libraries for Machine Learning and AI
- **Chapter 28:** Simulation and Test Environments for Agents
- **Chapter 29:** Frameworks for Multi-Agent Systems and Agent-Based Modeling
- **Chapter 30:** Development Tools: IDEs, Debugging and Version Control
- **Chapter 31:** Platforms for chatbots and voice assistants
- **Chapter 32:** Cloud Services and AI APIs (pre-built AI functions)

Part V: Ethical and social aspects

- **Chapter 33:** Ethical Foundations of AI Development
- **Chapter 34:** Responsible Design of AI Agents
- **Chapter 35:** Social Impacts of AI Agents: Opportunities and Risks
- **Chapter 36:** Detecting and avoiding bias and discrimination in AI systems
- **Chapter 37:** Transparency and Explainability of AI Systems
- **Chapter 38:** Data protection and security in AI applications
- **Chapter 39:** Legal framework and guidelines for AI

Part VI: Use cases in different areas

- **Chapter 40:** AI Agents in Robotics and Industry 4.0
- **Chapter 41:** AI agents in traffic and logistics (autonomous vehicles)
- **Chapter 42:** AI Agents in Computer Games and Simulations
- **Chapter 43:** AI Agents in Medicine and Healthcare
- **Chapter 44:** AI Agents in Finance
- **Chapter 45:** AI Agents in Customer Service and Marketing
- **Chapter 46:** AI agents in everyday life: Smart homes and personal assistants
- **Chapter 47:** AI Agents in Education and E-Learning

Part VII: Future Perspectives and Trends

- **Chapter 48:** Current Trends in AI Agent Development
- **Chapter 49:** Future developments and visions for AI agents
- **Chapter 50:** Conclusion and Outlook

Chapter 1: What is Artificial Intelligence? Introduction and Basic Concepts

1.1 Introduction

Artificial intelligence (AI) is one of the most significant technological developments of our time. It influences numerous areas of life, from smartphones to autonomous driving to complex medical diagnoses. But what exactly is behind the term "artificial intelligence"? How do different types of AI differ and which basic concepts are essential for understanding them?

This chapter explains the basic terms and concepts of artificial intelligence. The aim is to create a solid foundation on which later chapters can build. We will look at both the historical development and key use cases.

1.2 Definition of Artificial Intelligence

The term "artificial intelligence" is broad and has various definitions that vary depending on the context. Basically, artificial intelligence describes a branch of computer science that deals with the development of machines or systems that can perform human-like intelligence tasks.

One of the generally accepted definitions comes from John McCarthy, a pioneer in AI research:

"Artificial intelligence is the science and technology of producing intelligent machines, especially intelligent computer programs." (McCarthy, 1956)

AI encompasses numerous sub-areas such as machine learning, neural networks, expert systems and natural language processing. It is not just a purely technical concept, but also an interdisciplinary research area that is linked to psychology, mathematics, philosophy and neuroscience.

1.2.1 Weak vs. strong AI

A central concept in AI research is the distinction between *weak* and *strong* AI.

- **Weak AI : This form of AI is specialized for specific tasks and** cannot imitate general human intelligence. Examples include voice assistants such as Siri or Google Assistant , which process natural language but do not have true understanding.

- **Strong AI** : This form of AI would have human-like intelligence that is not only designed for specific problems, but could think and learn flexibly in different contexts. Strong AI currently only exists in theory and is a long-term goal of AI research.

1.3 Historical Development of Artificial Intelligence

Research into artificial intelligence goes back several decades. The most important milestones in this development can be divided into different phases.

1.3.1 The beginnings of AI (1950s - 1970s)

The first concepts of AI emerged in the 1950s. The mathematician Alan Turing developed the famous *Turing Test* , a procedure for evaluating whether a machine exhibits intelligent behavior. In 1956, the term "artificial intelligence" was officially coined during the Dartmouth Conference.

Important developments of this time:

- 1950: Alan Turing's article *Computing Machinery and Intelligence* asks the question "Can machines think?"
- 1956: Dartmouth Conference → Birth of AI as a research field
- 1966: Joseph Weizenbaum's ELIZA, one of the first chatbot systems

1.3.2 AI winter and machine learning (1980s - 1990s)

After initial enthusiasm, AI research experienced a setback in the 1970s because expectations were not met. A lack of computing power and inadequate algorithms led to little progress. It was not until the 1980s that new optimism was sparked with the advent of expert systems.

- 1980s: Expert systems become popular (e.g. medical diagnostic programs)
- 1997: IBM's *Deep Blue* beats world chess champion Garry Kasparov

1.3.3 The modern era of AI (2000s - present)

With the exponential increase in computing power, large amounts of data (big data) and improved algorithms, AI has experienced revolutionary progress in the last two decades. Machine learning and especially deep neural networks are the driving forces behind modern AI systems.

- 2011: IBM Watson wins the quiz show *Jeopardy!*
- 2016: DeepMind's AlphaGo beats the world's best Go player
- Today: Autonomous vehicles, voice assistants and generative AI models (e.g. ChatGPT) are ubiquitous

1.4 Sub-areas of Artificial Intelligence

AI is a broad research field that includes various sub-areas:

1.4.1 Machine Learning (ML)

Machine learning is a subfield of AI in which algorithms recognize patterns from data and make predictions on their own. There are three main types of machine learning:

- *Supervised learning* : The model learns from labeled data (e.g. pictures of cats and dogs).

- *Unsupervised learning* : The model independently finds patterns in data (e.g. customer segmentation).

- *Reinforcement learning* : The model learns through rewards and punishments (e.g. robot control).

1.4.2 Neural Networks and Deep Learning

Neural networks are inspired by the structure of the human brain and consist of artificial neurons. Deep learning uses deep neural networks with many layers and is responsible for advances in computer vision and language processing.

1.4.3 Natural Language Processing (NLP)

NLP enables machines to understand, interpret and generate human language. Applications include:

- voice assistants (Siri, Alexa)

- translation software (Google Translate)

- chatbots and text generators

1.4.4 Robotics and autonomous systems

The combination of AI with robotics enables machines to act autonomously in the physical world. Examples include:

- Autonomous vehicles (e.g. Tesla, Waymo)

- Industrial robots in manufacturing

- service robots for household and care

Chapter 2: Intelligent Agents – Definition and Examples

2.1 Introduction

Artificial intelligence (AI) is a broad field that encompasses many different concepts and technologies. One of the most fundamental ideas in AI is that of the *intelligent agent* . Intelligent agents are autonomous systems that operate in an environment, processing perceptions, making decisions, and executing actions. They form the foundation of many AI applications, from search engines to autonomous vehicles.

In this chapter we will discuss in detail the definition of intelligent agents, their structure and various examples from theory and practice.

2.2 What is an intelligent agent?

An *intelligent agent* is a system that perceives its environment and performs actions based on it to achieve certain goals. This can range from simple rule-based systems to highly complex, self-learning algorithms.

2.2.1 Definition of an intelligent agent

The term "agent" comes from computer science and refers to an autonomous system that can interact with its environment. An intelligent agent has the following essential properties:

- **Perception : The agent receives information from its environment (** e.g. through sensors, cameras or data streams).

- **Processing** : The recorded information is analyzed and interpreted.

- **Decision -making :** Based on the analysis, the agent makes a decision about which action to perform.

- **Action (Action- taking)** : The agent performs the chosen action (e.g. a movement, a calculation or a communication with other systems).

2.2.2 Basic model of an intelligent agent

An agent can generally be described by the following model:

$$\text{Agent} = (\text{Sensors}, \text{Effectors}, \text{Perception}, \text{Target}, \text{Environment})$$

Components of an agent:

- **Sensors** : Collect data from the environment (e.g. cameras, microphones, temperature sensors).

- **Effectors** : Execute actions (e.g. motors in robots, screen outputs in software agents).

- **Agent program** : Determines the agent's behavior based on its perceptions.

- **Objective** : The purpose or mission of the agent.

- **Environment** : The context in which the agent operates (e.g. a game, a city, the Internet).

2.2.3 A simple example: The vacuum cleaner agent

A classic example of an intelligent agent is an autonomous robot vacuum cleaner. It perceives its environment (e.g. through sensors for dirt or obstacles), decides on its next action (e.g. cleaning or changing direction) and executes it.

2.3 Types of intelligent agents

Intelligent agents can be divided into different categories depending on their complexity and behavior.

2.3.1 Simple reflex-based agents

These agents work according to the *perception → action principle* , without considering the past or complex calculations. They only react to current inputs.

📌 **Example:** A thermostat measures the room temperature and turns the heating on or off based on a predefined threshold.

2.3.2 Model-based reflex-based agents

These agents have an internal model of their environment that helps them make better decisions.

📌 **Example:** An intelligent vacuum cleaner that remembers where it has already cleaned.

2.3.3 Goal-based agents

These agents pursue explicit goals and choose actions that contribute to goal achievement.

📌 **Example:** A navigation system that calculates a route to reach a destination as quickly as possible.

2.3.4 Utility-based agents

These agents consider not only a goal but also a utility function to select the "best" action.

📌 **Example:** An autonomous vehicle that wants to reach its destination not only quickly but also safely.

2.3.5 Learning Agents

These agents improve their behavior through experience and machine learning.

📌 **Example:** A chess program that improves its strategy by playing many games.

2.4 Multi-agent systems

In many real-world applications, agents do not work in isolation, but rather collaborate with other agents in an environment or compete against each other. These systems are called *multi-agent systems* .

2.4.1 Properties of multi-agent systems

- **Cooperation** : Agents work together on a task (e.g. swarm intelligence in robotics).
- **Competition** : Agents operate in an adversarial environment (e.g. financial markets, chess AI).
- **Communication** : Agents exchange information to make better decisions.

📌 **Example:** Autonomous vehicles on the road that communicate with each other to avoid accidents.

2.5 Practical applications of intelligent agents

Intelligent agents can be found in many areas of technology. Here are some common use cases:

2.5.1 Virtual Assistants

Modern voice assistants such as Siri, Alexa and Google Assistant are learning agents that process language, respond to requests and perform actions.

2.5.2 Autonomous vehicles

Vehicles like Tesla or Waymo use AI agents to analyze their environment, make decisions and drive safely.

2.5.3 Financial markets

Trading algorithms use AI agents to analyze market data and make buy and sell decisions in real time.

2.5.4 Robotics

Modern robots in industry, healthcare and homes use intelligent agents to perform complex tasks autonomously.

2.5.5 Computer games

AI agents in computer games control NPCs (non-player characters), adapt to the players' behavior and provide a challenging gaming experience.

Intelligent agents are a fundamental component of artificial intelligence. They enable machines to make decisions independently and act in different environments. The development of agents ranges from simple rule-based systems to complex, self-learning algorithms.

Chapter 3: History of AI and the Development of Agents

3.1 Introduction

The history of artificial intelligence (AI) and the development of intelligent agents is a fascinating journey through decades of research and technological innovation. The idea of creating machines with human-like thinking abilities goes back a long way, but it was not until the mid-20th century that modern AI research began.

This chapter provides an overview of the most important milestones in AI development and shows how intelligent agents have evolved from simple rule-based systems to powerful, learning systems.

3.2 The early concepts and philosophical foundations

The idea of machines that can think and act has existed since ancient times. Myths and stories have described artificial beings that serve or challenge humans.

3.2.1 Antiquity and the Middle Ages

- In Greek mythology, the god Hephaestus created mechanical servants made of metal that acted independently.

- The philosopher Aristotle developed *formal logic* , a basis for later AI systems.

- In the Middle Ages there were mechanical automatons that could perform simple movements but did not have any real intelligence.

3.2.2 Early mathematical and logical foundations (17th–19th centuries)

With the development of mathematics and logic, the first formal approaches to modeling thinking and decision-making were created:

- **René Descartes (17th century)** investigated the idea of mechanical bodies and rational souls.

- **Gottfried Wilhelm Leibniz (18th century)** developed a concept for a "logic machine" that could systematically calculate arguments.

- **George Boole (19th century)** invented *Boolean logic* , which later became the basis for digital circuits and AI.

3.3 The birth of modern AI (20th century)

3.3.1 Alan Turing and the first vision of AI (1936–1950)

- **Alan Turing** developed the concept of the *Turing machine* , a theoretical model for algorithmic thinking.

- In 1950 he introduced the *Turing test* , a criterion for evaluating the intelligence of a machine.

3.3.2 The Dartmouth Conference and the Birth of AI Research (1956)

- In 1956, the **Dartmouth Conference took** place, which is considered the official starting point of AI research. Scientists such as John McCarthy and Marvin Minsky coined the term "artificial intelligence" here.

- First programs like *Logic Theorist* and *General Problem Solver* were developed, but could only solve simple problems.

3.4 First AI systems and the AI winter (1960s–1980s)

3.4.1 Progress in the 1960s and 1970s

- The first rule-based systems were developed, including expert systems such as *DENDRAL* (for chemical analysis) and *MYCIN* (for medical diagnosis).

- Optimism in AI research was high, but hardware and memory limitations placed strict limits on what was possible.

3.4.2 The first AI winter (1974–1980)

- Governments and companies lost confidence in AI research because many promises were not kept .
- Funding for AI projects has been severely cut.

3.5 The Age of Machine Learning (1980s–2000s)

3.5.1 Resurgence of AI through expert systems (1980s)

- As computers improved, expert systems became popular and were used in fields such as medicine and industry.
- However, these systems proved to be too rigid and difficult to scale.

3.5.2 The second AI winter (1987–1993)

- Again, many projects were discontinued because expert systems could not meet expectations.
- At the same time, the concept of *neural networks was* revived, which later turned out to be revolutionary.

3.5.3 The breakthrough of deep learning (2000s–2010s)

- **Deep Blue** defeated world chess champion Garry Kasparov, a significant milestone.
- In the 2000s, advances in computing power and data availability led to the renaissance of machine learning.
- Algorithms such as *support vector machines* and *random forests* significantly improved AI systems.

3.6 Intelligent Agents and their Development

3.6.1 From rule-based agents to be learned

- Early intelligent agents were often rule-based, meaning they followed set rules to respond to inputs.
- With the advancement of machine learning, agents began to improve themselves through experience.

3.6.2 Multi-agent systems and networked AI

- In the 2000s, **multi-agent systems emerged** in which several agents cooperate or compete.
- This led to breakthroughs in areas such as simulations, financial markets and autonomous vehicles.

3.6.3 AI agents in the modern world (2010–present)

- **2011:** IBM's **Watson** won the quiz show *Jeopardy!* against human champions.

- **2016:** DeepMind's *AlphaGo* defeated the world's best Go player, which is considered a milestone in deep learning.

- **Today:** AI agents control vehicles, automate processes and assist in everyday life.

Chapter 4: AI agents in everyday life: current applications

4.1 Introduction

Artificial intelligence has gained enormous importance in recent years and is no longer an abstract concept that only exists in research laboratories or high-tech companies. AI agents accompany us every day, often without us consciously noticing it. From voice assistants to personalized advertising to self-driving cars - intelligent systems are omnipresent and are changing our lives for the better.

In this chapter, we take a detailed look at the most important applications of AI agents in everyday life and how they shape different industries and areas of life.

4.2 Digital assistants and voice control

One of the most visible and widely used AI agents is the digital voice assistant. Systems like Siri, Google Assistant and Alexa have revolutionized the way people interact with technology. Instead of pressing buttons or navigating menus, users can simply ask questions or speak commands.

These assistants use technologies such as natural language processing (NLP) and machine learning to understand language, interpret it in context, and provide appropriate responses. The more often a user interacts with the assistant, the better it adapts to individual habits. This shows how modern AI agents not only provide predefined responses, but also learn and continuously improve their performance.

In addition to general information searches, digital assistants are also playing an increasingly important role in households. Smart speakers make it possible to control devices, play music, manage shopping lists or set reminders. Networking with smart home technologies is continually expanding these possible uses.

4.3 AI agents in conversation

Artificial intelligence is also widely used in the entertainment sector. Streaming services such as Netflix, Spotify and YouTube use intelligent algorithms to provide personalized recommendations. These systems analyze user behavior, learn preferences and suggest content that is likely to be liked.

AI agents also play a central role in the video game industry. In modern games, computer-controlled characters are often equipped with self-learning algorithms that dynamically adapt their behavior. This creates more realistic game worlds and more intelligent opponents that adapt to the user's playing style.

In addition, AI-powered media editing tools enable completely new creative possibilities. Software can automatically compose music, generate images or optimize videos, giving even non-experts access to sophisticated technologies.

4.4 AI in the financial world

The financial industry uses AI agents in a variety of ways. One of the best-known applications is the automatic analysis of financial markets. Algorithms evaluate large amounts of economic data and make lightning-fast trading decisions that are often more efficient than human analysts. This form of algorithmic trading now accounts for a significant portion of global stock market trading.

Another area of application is risk management. Banks and insurance companies use AI to assess creditworthiness, detect fraud attempts and offer customized financial products. Modern systems not only analyze classic financial data, but also include unusual patterns or behaviors in their calculations.

AI agents are also useful for consumers in the financial sector. Chatbots answer customer queries, automated advisors suggest investment options, and AI-powered apps help manage personal finances. This makes banking more efficient, more customer-friendly and often more secure.

4.5 Intelligent Agents in Medicine and Healthcare

The healthcare industry is experiencing profound change thanks to AI. AI agents are increasingly being used in diagnostics to detect diseases earlier and more precisely. Modern systems analyze medical images such as X-rays or MRI scans and identify abnormalities with high accuracy. Machine learning allows these systems to continuously learn and improve their detection rates.

Another important field of application is personalized medicine. AI agents analyze genetic information and individual disease progression to create customized treatment plans. This allows therapies to be better tailored to individual patients, which increases the chances of recovery.

AI is also playing a growing role in patient care. Intelligent chatbots answer medical questions, virtual health assistants remind patients to take their medication, and algorithms support doctors in making complex decisions. In addition, robot-assisted surgical systems enable more precise interventions by stabilizing and optimizing human movements.

4.6 AI in transport and logistics

Autonomous vehicles are one of the most ambitious applications for AI agents. Companies like Tesla, Waymo and traditional automakers are working to develop vehicles that can drive themselves and make decisions in real time, using a variety of sensors, cameras and neural networks to analyze the environment and calculate safe driving strategies.

AI agents have also become indispensable in the logistics industry. They optimize routes, calculate the most efficient use of transport and improve supply chain coordination. Through predictive analysis, companies can optimize the flow of goods and avoid bottlenecks.

In aviation, AI agents are increasingly taking over tasks in air traffic control and maintenance. Intelligent systems analyze weather data, traffic patterns and aircraft status reports to minimize delays and increase safety.

4.7 Smart household appliances and AI in everyday life

In the home environment, AI agents make numerous everyday tasks easier. Smart household appliances learn from users and adapt to individual preferences. Modern thermostats analyze heating behavior and automatically regulate the room temperature to save energy. Refrigerators can monitor inventory and make shopping suggestions.

AI also plays a major role in security technology. Intelligent surveillance systems analyze movement patterns and detect unusual activities. Facial recognition systems enable personalized access control, and smart door locks can be conveniently controlled via voice command or app.

Personal assistance systems are also increasingly being equipped with AI capabilities. From automated email filters to appointment planners that optimize the daily routine - AI agents are fundamentally changing everyday life.

4.8 Conclusion

AI agents are no longer a vision of the future, but an integral part of everyday life. They facilitate communication, optimize work processes, improve healthcare and increase efficiency in many areas. The systems are constantly evolving and opening up new possibilities.

However, the rapid development also presents challenges. Data protection, ethical questions and the increasing automation of human activities are key issues that must continue to be discussed. Despite these challenges, it is clear that AI agents will continue to play a crucial role in our daily lives in the future.

In the next chapter, we turn to the theoretical foundations of intelligent agents and examine the concepts that determine how they work.

Part II: Theoretical Foundations of AI Agents

Chapter 5: Fundamentals of Intelligent Agents – Perception, Actions and Environment

5.1 Introduction

Intelligent agents are systems that can autonomously make decisions and perform actions in their environment. They are the foundation of many AI applications, from autonomous vehicles to robotics to software agents used in areas such as finance or medicine.

To understand an agent's behavior, it is important to consider its three central components: perception, action, and environment. In this chapter, we will analyze these concepts in detail and explain how they work together to enable intelligent decision making.

5.2 Perception: The way agents perceive their environment

Every intelligent agent needs a way to perceive its environment. This perception occurs through sensors or input sources that collect physical or digital data.

For example, a physical robot can use cameras, microphones or temperature sensors to analyze its environment. A software agent, on the other hand, collects information from databases, websites or user requests.

The quality of perception depends on several factors. First, **sensor resolution plays** a role, as high-resolution sensors can provide more precise data. Second, **data processing speed is** crucial, as an agent must make quick decisions when acting in real time, for example in an autonomous vehicle.

There are two main categories of perception:

1. **Direct perception:** The agent receives raw sensor data and processes it itself. An example would be a camera system that evaluates visual information to detect obstacles.

2. **Derived perception:** Here the agent uses information that has already been processed. For example, a navigation system uses an existing road map instead of mapping the environment itself.

Another important concept is the **incompleteness of perception** . No agent can perceive its environment 100% because sensors are limited and often only represent a part of reality. Therefore, intelligent agents must deal with uncertainty and improve their perception through models or probabilistic methods.

5.3 Action: How agents make decisions and influence their environment

After an agent perceives its environment, it must select an appropriate action. This process can range from simple, predefined rules to complex decision models based on machine learning.

Actions can be divided into different categories:

- **Deterministic actions:** The agent always chooses the same action for a given situation. For example, a thermostat turns on the heating as soon as the temperature falls below a certain value.

- **Stochastic actions:** The agent's decision involves a probability. An autonomous vehicle at an intersection might choose a route with the highest probability of arriving quickly.

- **Planned actions:** Here, a sequence of actions is calculated to achieve a long-term goal. For example, a logistics agent optimizes the order of goods deliveries to minimize transport time.

Decisions can be based on different principles. Rule-based systems follow simple if-then rules, while learning systems optimize based on past experience. In advanced systems, mathematical models such as reinforcement learning or Bayesian networks are used to calculate probabilities and rewards.

Another distinction is between reactive and deliberative agents. Reactive agents react immediately to environmental changes, without long-term planning. A simple reflex-based vacuum cleaner robot falls into this category. Deliberative agents, on the other hand, create a strategy by simulating and evaluating various possible future scenarios.

5.4 Environment: The environment in which an agent operates

The environment of an agent largely determines how complex its tasks are and which strategies it must use. An environment can be structured differently and brings with it different challenges.

First, an environment is either fully or incompletely observable. In a game of chess, the AI agent knows the entire playing field and all possible moves, so the environment is fully observable. In road traffic, however, an autonomous vehicle has only limited information, for example from cameras and sensors, and must deal with uncertainties such as sudden obstacles.

Furthermore, an environment can be deterministic or stochastic. Deterministic environments have predictable rules, as is the case with chess or many industrial automation systems. Stochastic environments contain random factors, such as weather conditions for a delivery drone system or the behavior of other road users.

Another important aspect is the dynamic nature of the environment. An agent operating in a static environment, such as an image processing algorithm, can work with fixed data. An agent in a dynamic environment, such as a robot in a factory, must continuously adapt its decisions as its environment is constantly changing.

The number of agents involved also plays a role. In a single-agent environment, the agent acts alone, while in a multi-agent environment it must interact with other agents. In networked systems, such as autonomous delivery drones, the agents must coordinate with each other to avoid collisions and act efficiently.

5.5 Interaction of perception, action and environment

Intelligent agents rely on balancing perception, actions and their environment to make effective decisions. Poor or faulty perception can lead to wrong decisions, while a suboptimal action strategy remains inefficient despite good sensing.

A practical example is an autonomous vehicle. The sensors continuously perceive the environment and identify road signs, pedestrians and other vehicles. Based on this information, the control algorithm calculates the best course of action, be it braking, accelerating or avoiding an obstacle.

Another example is an AI-powered customer service chatbot. It perceives the questions entered, analyzes the meaning and decides on the best answer or forwards to a human advisor. The quality of its perception directly influences the usefulness of its answers.

To further improve the behavior of intelligent agents, a feedback loop is often implemented. The agent uses the effects of its own actions to optimize its behavior. Reinforcement learning systems train themselves by trying out different action strategies and adapting their future decisions based on the successes or failures achieved.

5.6 Conclusion

Perception, action and environment are the three pillars of intelligent agents. They determine how an agent interprets its environment, which actions it chooses and which challenges it must overcome.

The design of these components depends heavily on the specific application. While some agents work in structured, predictable environments, others need to act flexibly in highly dynamic scenarios.

Chapter 6: Types of AI Agents – Reflexive, Goal-Oriented and Utility-Based Agents

6.1 Introduction

Intelligent agents can be divided into different categories depending on their structure and decision-making mechanism. Choosing the right type of agent depends heavily on the complexity of the environment and the goals of the system. This chapter examines three central types of AI agents: reflex-based agents, goal-oriented agents, and utility-based agents.

These agent types differ in their ability to process information from the environment, pursue goals, and optimize decisions. While simple reflex-based agents react directly to environmental influences, utility-based agents make strategic decisions based on probabilities and utility evaluations.

6.2 Reflex-based agents

Reflex-based agents are the simplest form of intelligent agents. They are based on a direct connection between perception and action, without the need for complex calculations or strategic planning. These agents work according to the "if-then" principle, meaning they follow fixed rules or patterns that determine which action is carried out in a given situation.

6.2.1 Properties of reflex-based agents

These agents are particularly efficient in well-structured environments where clear rules for actions exist. Since they do not perform deep analysis or planning, they can work quickly and with minimal computational effort.

A disadvantage of these agents is their limited flexibility. They can only react to predefined situations and are not able to adapt to new, unknown scenarios. In dynamic or unpredictable environments, they quickly reach their limits.

6.2.2 Examples of reflex-based agents

A classic example of a reflex-based agent is a thermostat. It measures the temperature in a room and reacts immediately to deviations from a preset value by turning the heating on or off.

Another example is a robot vacuum cleaner that uses simple obstacle sensors. When it encounters an obstacle, it changes direction without performing a comprehensive analysis of the environment.

In the digital world, spam filters in email systems are also reflex-based agents. They follow predefined rules to classify incoming messages, for example based on certain keywords or sender addresses.

6.3 Goal-oriented agents

While reflex-based agents merely react to environmental stimuli, goal-oriented agents pursue a long-term plan. They choose their actions not only based on current perceptions, but also based on a higher-level goal.

6.3.1 Properties of goal-oriented agents

Goal-oriented agents use an internal representation of their goal to strategically select actions. They analyze their environment and calculate the steps necessary to achieve a specific goal.

A major advantage of these agents is their flexibility. Since they not only react to immediate environmental influences, but also align their actions with the achievement of a goal, they can also survive in more complex scenarios. However, they often require more computing power because they have to evaluate different options for action.

6.3.2 Examples of goal-oriented agents

A navigation system in a car is a typical example of a goal-oriented agent. It calculates the optimal route to a given destination and adjusts the direction of travel depending on traffic conditions.

Another example is autonomous drones that carry out deliveries. They analyze weather conditions, airspace restrictions and energy consumption to find the most efficient route to the destination.

Modern chatbots are also often goal-oriented agents. Instead of just giving ready-made answers to certain inputs, they analyze the user's intent and steer the conversation in such a way that a meaningful interaction with the desired result occurs.

6.4 Utility-based agents

Utility-based agents go beyond pure goal pursuit and evaluate different options for action based on a utility model. They consider not only whether a goal is achieved, but also *how good* a particular action is compared to other possible options.

6.4.1 Properties of utility-based agents

A utility-based agent uses what is called a *utility function* , which assigns a value to each possible action. This function can be based on various criteria, including efficiency, safety, or speed.

A key advantage of these agents is their ability to operate under uncertainty. While a goal-oriented agent may only be focused on achieving a specific goal, a utility-based agent can weigh between several options and choose the one with the highest expected utility.

6.4.2 Examples of utility-based agents

Autonomous vehicles use utility-based decision models to develop optimal driving strategies. They evaluate not only which route is the shortest, but also factors such as safety, traffic flow and energy consumption.

Another example is online advertising algorithms that deliver personalized ads. Instead of simply showing ads for random products, utility-based agents calculate the likelihood that a user will respond to an ad and choose the most profitable option accordingly .

In the financial world, utility-based agents are used in algorithmic trading. They analyze market data and make investment decisions based on a utility function that takes into account factors such as risk, profit potential and market volatility.

6.5 Comparison of agent types

The choice between reflex-based, goal-oriented and utility-based agents depends largely on the application. Reflex-based agents are particularly efficient for simple, predictable tasks with fixed rules. Goal-oriented agents are suitable for more dynamic environments in which decisions must be made based on a long-term plan. Utility-based agents are the most flexible systems because they can weigh up different courses of action against each other and thus always make the best decision.

In practice, many modern AI systems are a combination of several agent types. An autonomous vehicle, for example, uses reflex-based mechanisms for emergency braking, goal-oriented algorithms for navigation, and utility-based decision models for optimizing driving strategies.

6.6 Conclusion

Choosing the right agent architecture is crucial for the success of an AI application. Reflex-based agents offer speed and simplicity, but are often inadequate in complex scenarios. Goal-oriented agents enable more flexible and strategic decision-making processes, while utility-based agents offer an optimal balance between efficiency and goal achievement.

The next stage of development is learning agents that can develop new strategies from experience and adapt dynamically to changing environments.

Chapter 7: Learning Agents – Introduction to Machine Learning

7.1 Introduction

Learning agents are one of the most powerful developments in the field of artificial intelligence. While simple agents are based on predefined rules, learning agents can adapt and improve their behavior by learning from experience. They are able to recognize patterns, make predictions and develop optimal decisions independently.

At the heart of learning agents is **machine learning (ML)** , a method in which algorithms learn from data rather than being explicitly programmed. This approach has led to revolutionary advances in numerous fields in recent years, from natural language processing to autonomous vehicles.

In this chapter, we look at the fundamentals of machine learning, the different learning paradigms, and the challenges associated with training learning agents.

7.2 Basics of Machine Learning

Machine learning is a subfield of artificial intelligence that deals with the development of algorithms that can learn from data and automatically adapt their behavior.

7.2.1 How does machine learning work?

Instead of using an explicit list of rules, a learning agent analyzes large amounts of sample data and recognizes patterns. These patterns are stored in a **model** that is then used for prediction or decision making.

A learning agent requires three central components:

1. **Data** : The basis for training, such as images, text or sensor values.

2. **Model** : A mathematical structure that extracts and stores patterns from the data.

3. **Learning algorithm** : A method that trains and adapts the model to produce better results.

7.2.2 Training and optimization

Learning agents go through several stages during the training process. First, the model is fed with a large amount of data. The learning algorithm then adjusts the model's internal parameters to find the best match between inputs and desired outputs.

Training can be supervised or unsupervised. In many cases, an **error measure is** used to determine how well the agent has learned. Through iterative adjustments, the model is optimized until errors are minimized and performance is satisfactory.

7.3 Types of machine learning

There are different methods to train learning agents. The three main approaches are supervised learning, unsupervised learning and reinforcement learning.

7.3.1 Supervised Learning

In supervised learning, the agent trains on examples with known inputs and outputs. It is given a set of data in which each input has a correct target output. The algorithm tries to learn a function that can generalize these mappings.

A classic example is handwriting recognition. A model is trained with images of letters, each with its correct label (e.g. "A", "B", "C"). After sufficient training, the agent can recognize new letters, even if it has not seen them before.

7.3.2 Unsupervised Learning

Unlike supervised learning, unsupervised learning does not provide predetermined target outputs. Instead, the algorithm analyzes the data to identify patterns or structures.

A common use case is **clustering** . For example, an algorithm could analyze customer data to identify groups with similar purchasing habits. These clusters can then be used for personalized advertising or targeted product offers.

7.3.3 Reinforcement Learning (RL)

In reinforcement learning, an agent interacts with its environment and learns through reward or punishment. The goal is to find an optimal strategy that brings the greatest benefit in the long term.

This approach is often used for complex decision problems where a direct mapping between inputs and outputs is difficult to define. An example is an autonomous robot that moves through an unknown environment and receives rewards for making correct decisions, such as successfully avoiding an obstacle or efficiently completing a task.

7.4 Machine Learning in Practice

Learning agents are now used in many areas of everyday life.

7.4.1 Speech recognition and translations

Voice assistants such as Siri or Google Assistant use machine learning to understand spoken language and convert it into text. Through continuous training with large amounts of speech data, these systems are becoming increasingly precise.

Automatic translations are also based on learning agents. Modern translation systems analyze huge amounts of text in different languages and recognize complex linguistic patterns.

7.4.2 Image processing and object recognition

In medicine, AI-supported systems analyze X-ray and MRI images to detect diseases at an early stage. Similar technologies are used in the security industry, for example for facial recognition or to identify suspicious activities in surveillance systems.

7.4.3 Recommendation systems

Streaming services such as Netflix or Spotify use learning agents to provide personalized recommendations. Based on previous usage data, these systems suggest films, series or music that match the user's individual taste.

7.4.4 Autonomous vehicles

Self-driving cars use machine learning to analyze traffic situations and navigate safely through traffic. These vehicles combine different learning methods to detect obstacles, interpret traffic signs and optimize driving strategies.

7.5 Challenges of Machine Learning

Despite the impressive progress, there are some challenges that must be considered when using machine learning.

7.5.1 Data quality and biases

A learning agent is only as good as the data it is trained with. Bad or distorted data can lead to wrong decisions. For example, facial recognition systems can have difficulty correctly identifying people of different skin colors if they have only been trained with a limited data set.

7.5.2 Explainability and transparency

Many ML models, especially neural networks, are so-called **"black box" systems** where it is difficult to understand how a particular decision was made. However, in safety-critical areas, such as medicine or finance, it is important that decisions are understandable and explainable.

7.5.3 Overfitting and Generalization

A common problem when training AI agents is **overfitting** – the model learns the training data too accurately and fails to generalize well to new data. This can result in an agent that works perfectly in a controlled environment but fails in real-world situations.

7.6 Conclusion

Learning agents are a key technology in modern AI. They enable machines to adapt to new challenges and continuously improve through experience. Machine learning has enabled enormous advances in areas such as speech recognition, image processing and autonomous driving.

Despite many successes, challenges remain, particularly in terms of data quality, transparency and generalizability. But as algorithms and hardware continue to evolve, learning agents will play an even greater role in the coming years.

Chapter 8: Problem Solving through Search – Basic Search Algorithms

8.1 Introduction

A central concept of intelligent agents is the ability to solve problems. In many cases, this means that an agent must search for a solution in a state space. The state space describes all possible configurations of a problem and their transitions.

Search algorithms are essential for a wide range of applications, from path planning in autonomous vehicles to strategic decision making in games. In this chapter, we will examine basic search methods and see how they help agents make optimal decisions.

8.2 Basics of Search in AI Systems

The search is about finding a path to a target state starting from a starting state. The agent moves step by step through the state space and evaluates possible solutions based on a defined criterion.

The choice of the right search algorithm depends on several factors, including the size of the search space, the availability of information about the problem, and the efficiency of the algorithm.

Most search algorithms fall into two main categories: uninformed (blind) search and informed (heuristic) search. Uninformed algorithms have no additional information about the problem and explore the state space systematically, while informed algorithms use knowledge about the problem to make the search more efficient.

8.3 Uninformed search algorithms

Uninformed search algorithms do not require any additional information about the structure of the problem. They are particularly useful when no heuristic is available or when all states are treated as equivalent.

8.3.1 Breadth -First Search (BFS)

Breadth-first search explores the state space step by step from the root in all directions. It first expands all immediate neighbors of a node before moving into deeper levels of the search space.

Properties of breadth-first search:

- Guarantees that the shortest solution is found (if all costs are equal).

- However, it can be very memory intensive as many nodes need to be stored simultaneously.

An example of BFS is the search for the shortest path in a maze by systematically exploring all possible movements.

8.3.2 Depth-First Search (DFS)

Depth-first search goes as deep into the state space as possible before backtracking and trying another path.

Properties of depth-first search:

- Requires less memory than breadth-first search because it only stores the current path.

- it can drift into deep, irrelevant branches and is not guaranteed to be optimal.

An example of DFS is browsing a file system by starting from a folder and navigating to the deepest directory level before returning.

8.3.3 Uniform Cost Search

Uniform Cost Search always expands the node with the lowest accumulated cost. This guarantees that the lowest cost solution is found, but the algorithm can be inefficient in very large search spaces.

An example is navigation in a road network, where not only the number of nodes (road intersections) but also their weighting (distance or travel time) is taken into account.

8.4 Informed search algorithms

Informed search algorithms use additional information about the problem to make the search more efficient. They use **heuristics** to select the "most promising" next state.

8.4.1 Greedy Best-First Search

This method always examines the node with the lowest estimated cost next. It uses a heuristic function that indicates how "close" a state is to the goal.

An example of this algorithm is navigation in a city map, where a vehicle always chooses the street with the shortest straight-line distance to the destination.

8.4.2 A-Algorithm *

The A algorithm * combines the advantages of the Uniform Cost Search and the Greedy Best-First Search. It takes into account both the previous costs and a heuristic to ensure the most efficient search possible.

A* uses the evaluation function:

$$f(n)=g(n)+h(n) \quad f(n) = g(n) + h(n) \quad f(n)=g(n)+h(n)$$

where:

- $g(n)$ $g(n)$ $g(n)$ is the actual cost from the start to the current node.

- $h(n)$ $h(n)$ $h(n)$ is an estimate of the remaining costs to the goal.

This combination guarantees that the best solution is found as long as the heuristic used is permissible.

A classic example of the A* algorithm is the calculation of the optimal route in a navigation system, which takes into account both the distance already traveled and the estimated remaining distance.

8.5 Comparison of search algorithms

The choice of the right search algorithm depends heavily on the specific problem. While uninformed search methods are often used in situations without additional information, heuristic algorithms enable more efficient search, especially in large state spaces.

Comparison of the most important algorithms:

algorithm	optimality	completeness	storage requirements	efficiency
breadth-first search (BFS)	Yes	Yes	High	Small amount
Depth-First Search (DFS)	No	No (except with iterative deepening)	Small amount	Medium
Uniform- Cost Search	Yes	Yes	High	Medium
Greedy Search	No	No	Medium	High
A* algorithm	Yes	Yes	Medium	High

Each of these algorithms has specific strengths and weaknesses, which is why hybrid methods are often developed to combine the best features of different approaches.

8.6 Practical Applications of Search Algorithms

Search algorithms are indispensable in many areas of artificial intelligence.

In robotics, autonomous robots use pathfinding algorithms to avoid obstacles and find the most efficient route to a destination.

In computer game development, search algorithms enable NPCs (non-player characters) to make smart moves or develop optimal strategies against human players.

In medical diagnostics, search algorithms are used to analyze possible clinical pictures and determine the most likely causes of a combination of symptoms.

Search processes also play a crucial role in logistics systems, for example in route planning for parcel deliveries or the optimization of warehousing systems.

8.7 Conclusion

Search algorithms are a fundamental tool for intelligent agents because they allow them to systematically search for optimal solutions in complex environments. Uninformed search methods are easy to implement but inefficient in large state spaces. Informed search algorithms such as A* offer a more powerful alternative by using additional knowledge to speed up the search.

Chapter 9: Heuristic Search and Optimization Methods

9.1 Introduction

In many real-world problems, the search space is too large to systematically explore all possibilities. While uninformed search algorithms such as breadth-first search (BFS) or depth-first search (DFS) are suitable for small search spaces, they prove to be inefficient for more complex problems.

This is where heuristic search comes into play. Heuristics are approximate methods that use additional information about the problem to guide the search. This allows the agent to preferentially explore promising paths and avoid inefficient paths.

In addition to heuristic search methods, there are optimization methods that aim to find not just any solution, but the most optimal solution possible. These methods play a crucial role in areas such as machine learning, robotics, logistics, and many other applications of artificial intelligence.

In this chapter, we examine various heuristic search algorithms and optimization techniques that help solve problems more efficiently.

9.2 Basics of heuristic search

A heuristic is an estimator that evaluates the quality of a state with respect to the desired goal. Instead of blindly navigating the search space, the heuristic guides the algorithm toward the most promising solutions.

Mathematically, a heuristic is represented as a function $h(n)h(n)h(n)$, which provides an estimate of the remaining cost to the goal for each node nnn .

9.2.1 Properties of a good heuristic

An effective heuristic should:

- **accurate** as possible and provide realistic estimates.

- **computationally efficient** so that it does not require more computational effort than the actual search.

- **permissible** , that is, it should never specify values that are too low to ensure that the solution found is really optimal.

A classic heuristic in navigation systems is the straight-line distance between the current location and the destination. Although the actual distance may be longer, this estimate provides a useful guide for the direction of the search.

9.3 Heuristic search algorithms

There are various algorithms that use heuristics to make the search process more efficient.

9.3.1 Greedy Best-First Search

This algorithm always chooses the node with the lowest heuristic value $h(n)h(n)h(n)$, i.e. the one that appears most promising.

Advantages:

- Often works quickly as it moves directly towards the target.
- Easy to implement.

Disadvantages:

- May reach dead ends or take detours by ignoring previous costs.
- Not guaranteed to be optimal.

9.3.2 A-Algorithm *

The *A algorithm* * improves Greedy Best-First Search by considering not only the estimated future costs $h(n)h(n)h(n)$, but also the actual past costs $g(n)g(n)g(n)$:

$$f(n)=g(n)+h(n)f(n) = g(n) + h(n)f(n)=g(n)+h(n)$$

So the algorithm not only examines what appears to be the best next step, but also takes into account how expensive it was to get there.

Advantages:

- Guarantees optimal solutions if the heuristic is admissible.
- Works efficiently in many applications.

Disadvantages:

- Can consume a lot of memory in large search spaces.
- Performance depends heavily on the quality of the heuristics.

The A* algorithm is widely used in **route planning, robotics and game AI** .

9.4 Optimization methods in AI

In addition to heuristic search, there are a variety of optimization methods that aim to find the best solutions to a problem. These methods are often used in scenarios where many possible solutions exist, but only a few are optimal.

9.4.1 Local search methods

Local search algorithms improve an existing solution incrementally instead of searching the entire search space.

Hill Climbing (mountain climbing algorithm)

This algorithm starts with a random solution and improves it through incremental adjustments. Whenever a better solution is found, it is adopted as the new starting solution.

Advantages:

- Very efficient for problems with many possible solutions.
- Easy to implement.

Disadvantages:

- Easily gets stuck in local optima (best solution in a small area, but not globally optimal).
- Cannot explore comprehensive search spaces.

An improvement of this algorithm is the Simulated Annealing , which allows occasional "bad" decisions to escape from local optima.

Tabu Search

This algorithm extends hill climbing by maintaining a taboo list that stores previously visited states. This allows it to avoid repeatedly entering the same area of the search space.

9.4.2 Evolutionary algorithms

Evolutionary algorithms are inspired by natural selection and are based on the principle of mutation and selection of solutions.

Genetic Algorithms (GA)

A genetic algorithm simulates an **evolutionary process** by generating a population of possible solutions and improving them through mechanisms such as **mutation, selection and recombination** .

Process:

1. A population of random solutions is created.
2. Each solution is evaluated (fitness function).
3. The best solutions are combined for the next generation.
4. Mutations are introduced to create new variants.
5. The process is repeated until an optimal solution is found.

Genetic algorithms are often used for **optimization problems** , for example in logistics for **route planning** or in the **financial sector** for portfolio management.

9.5 Comparison of search and optimization methods

Each method has its specific strengths and weaknesses. While **heuristic search algorithms** specifically look for solutions, **optimization methods are** designed to find the best possible solution.

method	type	Strengthen	Weaken
Greedy Best-First Search	Heuristic search	Fast, easy	Not guaranteed optimal
A* algorithm	Heuristic search	Optimal, efficient	High storage requirements
Hill Climbing	Local Search	Fast, practical	Remains stuck in local optima
Simulated annealing	Local Search	Bypasses local optima	Slower than Hill Climbing
Genetic algorithms	Evolutionary	Good for large search areas	Computationally intensive, requires many iterations

The choice of the right method depends strongly on the specific problem and the available computing resources.

9.6 Conclusion

Heuristic search methods and optimization algorithms are essential tools for AI agents to solve complex problems efficiently. While heuristic search helps to quickly find usable solutions, optimization methods enable the systematic improvement of solutions in order to determine the best variant.

Combining different methods, such as **hybrid algorithms** , can help to further improve efficiency and accuracy.

Chapter 10: Knowledge-Based Agents and Knowledge Representation

10.1 Introduction

While many AI agents operate through search algorithms and optimization techniques, there is another category of intelligent systems: knowledge-based agents. These agents use explicit knowledge about the world to make informed decisions.

In contrast to pure data-driven systems such as machine learning models, knowledge-based agents have an internal knowledge base that serves as the basis for logical reasoning. They can store rules, facts and concepts to solve problems and make rational decisions based on structured knowledge.

In this chapter, we consider how knowledge is formally represented, what types of knowledge representations exist, and how knowledge-based agents can make intelligent decisions through logical reasoning.

10.2 What are knowledge-based agents?

A knowledge-based agent is a system that stores and processes information and derives new insights from it. It consists of two main components:

1. **Knowledge Base (KB)**

    o   A collection of facts, rules and concepts about the world.

    o   Contains information in a structured form, such as logic rules or ontologies.

2. **inference engine**

    o   Uses logical rules to derive new information from existing knowledge.

    o   Decides which actions make sense based on the stored knowledge.

A knowledge-based agent can respond to a query by retrieving information from its knowledge base or drawing new conclusions.

For example, a medical expert system stores symptoms and diagnoses in its knowledge base. When a patient provides symptoms, the agent can suggest possible diagnoses based on this information.

10.3 Knowledge representation: How do agents store knowledge?

For an agent to work effectively, knowledge must be structured and stored in a form that can be processed by machines. There are various approaches to knowledge representation, each with advantages and disadvantages depending on the application.

10.3.1 Logic-based knowledge representation

Predicate logic is one of the most formal methods for knowledge representation. It is based on mathematical logic rules and allows precise conclusions.

- **Propositional logic:** Stores knowledge in the form of truth values (e.g. "All cats are mammals").

- **Predicate logic:** Uses variables and relations (e.g. *mammal(cat)*).

Advantages:

- High precision and formal correctness.

- Enables automatic reasoning.

Disadvantages:

- Complex knowledge structures are difficult to maintain.
- Scalability can be problematic.

10.3.2 Semantic Networks and Ontologies

A semantic network is a graph-based representation of knowledge in which nodes represent concepts and edges represent relations between these concepts.

Example:
A semantic network for animal classification could contain the following structure:

- "Dog is a mammal"
- "Mammal has lungs"
- "Dog has fur"

A more advanced model of this is ontologies, which formally describe hierarchical concepts and relationships. In computer science, ontologies are used, for example, in medical diagnostics to analyze complex clinical pictures.

Advantages:

- Enables structured knowledge processing.
- Good for semantic queries and relationships.

Disadvantages:

- Creating and maintaining an ontology requires a lot of effort.
- Can be difficult to adapt in dynamic systems.

10.3.3 Rule-based systems (if-then rules)

Rule-based systems store knowledge in the form of "if-then" rules.

Example:

- **Rule 1:** *If a patient has a fever and cough, he or she may have the flu.*
- **Rule 2:** *If flu is suspected, recommend medication.*

These rules enable direct decision-making without complex calculations. Such systems are often used in **expert systems** .

Advantages:

- Easy to understand and interpret.
- Well suited for expert systems.

Disadvantages:

- Rules can be contradictory or remain incomplete.
- As knowledge grows, the system becomes confusing.

10.4 Inference and logical reasoning in knowledge-based agents

A knowledge-based agent must not only store knowledge but also derive new knowledge. This is done through a mechanism that draws logical conclusions.

There are two main methods:

1. **forward chaining**

   o Start with known facts and derive new information from them.

   o Often used in expert systems.

Example:

   o Given: "All dogs are mammals" and "Bella is a dog."

   o Conclusion: "Bella is a mammal."

2. **Backward chaining (Backward Chaining)**

   o Start with a goal and work backwards to see if it can be supported by known facts.

   o Often used in diagnostic systems.

Example:

   o Goal: "Does the patient have the flu?"

   o Check if symptoms are consistent with flu.

An intelligent system can combine both methods to make informed decisions.

10.5 Applications of knowledge-based agents

Knowledge-based agents are used in many areas, including:

10.5.1 Medical diagnostic systems

Medical expert systems analyze patient data and suggest diagnoses based on known symptoms and treatment methods.

10.5.2 Legal expert systems

Legal agents analyze contracts or laws and make recommendations based on stored rules.

10.5.3 Industry and Automation

Knowledge-based agents are used for quality control or production planning in companies.

10.5.4 Search engines and recommendation systems

Search engines use semantic networks to provide users with relevant content based on previous search queries.

10.6 Challenges of knowledge-based agents

Despite their advantages, knowledge-based agents face challenges:

- **Knowledge acquisition and updating:** The creation and maintenance of knowledge bases is time-consuming.

- **Scalability:** Large amounts of knowledge can lead to complex and difficult to manage systems.

- **Incomplete knowledge:** Agents must deal with uncertainties and use probabilities if necessary.

To solve these problems, knowledge-based systems are increasingly being combined with machine learning so that they can automatically generate new knowledge.

10.7 Conclusion

Knowledge-based agents are essential components of many intelligent systems. They store explicit knowledge and use logical reasoning to solve problems. Depending on the application, different methods of knowledge representation can be used, including formal logic, semantic networks and rule-based systems.

Despite some challenges, knowledge-based agents have become indispensable in many industries. Thanks to advances in artificial intelligence and machine learning, these systems are becoming increasingly more powerful and flexible.

Chapter 11: Inference Mechanisms and Logical Reasoning

11.1 Introduction

Knowledge-based agents use stored knowledge not only to store information but also to derive new insights and make informed decisions. This process is called inference .

Inference mechanisms play a central role in many AI systems, especially in expert systems, diagnostic systems and automated decision-making processes. They enable an agent to derive new truths from known facts and rules, test hypotheses or evaluate situations.

This chapter covers the main techniques of logical reasoning, including deductive, inductive and abductive reasoning, and their applications in intelligent agents.

11.2 Basics of logical reasoning

Logical reasoning is a process by which new statements are derived from a set of given facts and rules. There are various methods of inference that are used depending on the problem.

11.2.1 Deductive reasoning

Deductive reasoning is based on formal logic and allows specific conclusions to be derived from general rules.

Example:

1. Rule: *All people are mortal.*

2. Fact: *Socrates is a human being.*

3. Conclusion: *Socrates is mortal.*

Deductive inference guarantees that the deduced statements are true as long as the premises are correct. It is often used in rule-based expert systems, mathematical logic, and legal decision-making systems.

11.2.2 Inductive closing

Inductive reasoning occurs through the recognition of patterns or probabilities. General rules are derived from specific observations.

Example:

1. Observation: *The sun rose today.*

2. Observation: *The sun rose yesterday.*

3. Conclusion: *The sun will rise again tomorrow.*

Induction is often used in machine learning, data analysis, and probabilistic systems because it allows generalizations to be made from existing data. However, there is always a risk that a conclusion is not correct in all cases.

11.2.3 Abductive reasoning

Abductive reasoning is used to find explanations for observed phenomena. It is not about deriving general rules, but rather about determining possible causes for a given observation .

Example:

1. Observation: *The ground is wet.*

2. Possible explanation: *It rained.*

Abduction is often used in medical diagnosis, forensic analysis, and error detection systems. It allows one to derive plausible causes from a given observation, but is not always unambiguous, as multiple explanations may be possible.

11.3 Inference mechanisms in knowledge-based agents

A knowledge-based agent needs a mechanism to draw logical conclusions from its stored knowledge. Various strategies are used for this purpose.

11.3.1 Forward Chaining

Forward chaining is a method in which the agent starts with known facts and gradually derives new information.

Example in an expert system:

- Fact: *Patient has cough and fever.*
- Rule: *If a patient has a cough and fever, he or she may have the flu.*
- Conclusion: *The patient may have the flu.*

This approach is often used in rule-based systems because it is easy to implement and builds gradually on new knowledge.

11.3.2 Backward chaining (Backward Chaining)

Backward chaining starts with a hypothesis or goal and checks whether it can be supported by existing facts.

Example:

- Objective: *Does the patient have the flu?*
- Rule: *If a patient has a cough and fever, he or she may have the flu.*
- Check: *Does the patient have a cough and fever?*
- If so, the hypothesis is confirmed.

This approach is often used in diagnostic systems and AI-based decision systems because it specifically looks for evidence for a hypothesis.

11.4 Probabilistic Reasoning

Not all AI systems work with exact rules. In many cases, agents have to deal with uncertainties and take probabilities into account.

11.4.1 Bayesian networks

Bayesian networks are probabilistic models that describe relationships between variables using probabilities.

Example in medical diagnosis:

- The likelihood that someone has the flu depends on symptoms such as fever and cough.
- The model calculates the probability of the disease based on existing symptoms and previous data.

Bayesian networks are used in **medical systems, financial models and risk analysis** .

11.4.2 Fuzzy logic

While classical logic only knows "true" or "false", fuzzy logic allows intermediate values.

Example:

- Temperature: *It is not just "hot" or "cold", but "moderately warm" or "slightly cool".*
- A washing machine can adjust the washing time depending on how dirty a garment is.

Fuzzy logic is often used in **control systems, household appliances and automation technology** .

11.5 Applications of logical reasoning in AI

Logical reasoning is used in numerous AI applications:

11.5.1 Medical diagnostic systems

Knowledge-based medical systems use inference mechanisms to make possible diagnoses based on symptoms.

11.5.2 Automatic planning and control

Industrial systems use logical reasoning to optimize production processes and control machines automatically.

11.5.3 AI in case law

Legal AI systems use logical rules to analyze contracts and support court decisions.

11.5.4 Speech processing and chatbots

Modern chatbots use logical rules and machine learning to conduct human-like conversations and intelligently generate answers.

11.6 Challenges of logical reasoning in AI

Although inference mechanisms are powerful, there are some challenges:

- **Complexity:** Logical reasoning can be computationally intensive for large knowledge bases.
- **Incompleteness:** Agents often have to deal with incomplete or contradictory information.
- **Explainability:** In many AI systems, it is difficult to understand how a particular conclusion was reached.

To address these challenges, hybrid approaches that combine **formal logic with machine learning and probabilistic methods are increasingly being used** .

11.7 Conclusion

Logical reasoning is an essential component of knowledge-based agents and enables the derivation of new information from known facts. Deductive, inductive and abductive reasoning offer different approaches to knowledge processing. While deterministic methods enable precise conclusions, probabilistic approaches and fuzzy logic allow the handling of uncertainties.

Modern AI systems often combine different inference mechanisms to make decisions flexibly and efficiently.

Chapter 12: Planning and Decision Making for Agents

12.1 Introduction

In many applications, intelligent agents are required not only to react to their environment but also to make planned decisions. While simple reflex-based agents perform immediate actions, advanced agents must act in advance to achieve optimal results in the long term.

Planning and decision-making are essential components of AI systems that operate in dynamic or uncertain environments. Autonomous robots, self-driving vehicles, game AI or logistics systems require sophisticated strategies to make optimal decisions.

This chapter deals with various methods of planning and decision making, including classical planning procedures, probabilistic decision models and modern learning-based approaches.

12.2 Basics of Planning in AI

Planning is the process by which an agent develops a sequence of actions to achieve a specific goal, taking into account possible future states of the environment to determine the best possible strategy.

A planning problem consists of the following elements:

- **State space** : A set of possible configurations of the environment.
- **Initial state** : The current state of the agent.
- **Goal state** : A desired state that the agent wants to achieve.
- **Actions** : A set of possible actions that can change the state.
- **Transition model** : Rules that describe how the environment changes as a result of an action.

Example: A robot is supposed to bring a certain product to a destination in a warehouse. The agent has to avoid various obstacles, minimize energy consumption and choose the shortest route.

Planning methods can be divided into **deterministic** and **stochastic** methods.

12.3 Classical planning methods

Classical planning methods assume that all states and actions are deterministic, i.e., every action leads to an exactly predictable result.

12.3.1 State space search

A simple approach to planning is to systematically search the entire state space. Methods such as *breadth-first search (BFS), depth-first search (DFS)* or *A-algorithm* * can be used to calculate optimal sequences of actions.

Example: A navigation system searches for the shortest route through a traffic network, assuming that road connections are reliable.

12.3.2 Planning graphs

A planning graph is a data structure that models states, actions and their effects. This method is often used in **AI planning systems** to search for possible solutions more efficiently.

12.3.3 Hierarchical planning

Hierarchical planning breaks a large problem down into smaller subproblems that can be solved separately. This reduces complexity and improves efficiency.

Example: An autonomous vehicle first plans a rough route (city $\rightarrow$ destination area) and then the exact driving strategy for individual road sections.

12.4 Uncertainty in decision-making

In many real-world applications, agents cannot fully understand their environment or make predictions. Weather conditions, unknown obstacles, or the behavior of other actors can complicate the planning process.

12.4.1 Probabilistic Planning

Probabilistic planning uses probability models to make decisions under uncertainty.

A common model is the **Markov Decision Process (Markov Decision Process , MDP)** , which is defined by the following elements:

- **States** : A set of possible world configurations.
- **Actions** : The actions the agent can perform.
- **Transition probabilities** : The probability with which an action leads to a certain state.
- **Reward function** : A rating that indicates how "good" a state is.

MDPs are widely used in robotics, financial decision making, and automated control systems.

12.4.2 Partially Observable Markov Decision Processes (POMDPs)

When an agent has only an incomplete perception of its environment, it uses POMDPs for decision making. These use probability distributions to select the best action based on uncertain knowledge.

Example: A rescue robot searches for survivors in a collapsed building without knowing exactly where obstacles or dangers are.

12.5 Benefit-based decision-making

Utility-based decision models evaluate different options for action using a utility function that indicates how advantageous a particular outcome is for the agent.

12.5.1 Decision trees

A decision tree graphically represents possible future events and helps identify the best option.

Example: A financial advisor can use a decision tree to analyze whether it is better to invest in a risky but potentially lucrative investment or to choose a safer alternative.

12.5.2 Expected Value Maximization

Agents calculate the **expected utility** of an action based on possible outcomes and their probabilities. They then choose the action with the highest expected utility.

Example: An autonomous vehicle considers whether to stop at a red light or drive carefully in the event of a medical emergency.

12.6 Machine Learning in Decision Making

Modern AI agents combine planning methods with machine learning to adaptively improve their strategies.

12.6.1 Reinforcement Learning (RL)

In reinforcement learning, an agent interacts with its environment and receives rewards for good decisions. Through many repetitions, it learns to develop optimal strategies.

A well-known example of RL is **AlphaGo** , an AI that learned through self-training to master the complex board game Go.

12.6.2 Deep Reinforcement Learning

It uses neural networks to solve high-dimensional decision problems. Deep RL is used in **robotics, game AI and autonomous systems** .

Example: A self-driving car uses Deep RL to learn safe driving strategies in complex environments.

12.7 Applications of planning and decision models

Planning and decision-making mechanisms are indispensable in numerous AI applications:

- **Robotics** : Industrial robots calculate optimal movements for assembling components.

- **Autonomous vehicles** : Self-driving cars use decision-making algorithms for navigation.

- **Game AI** : AI agents in games plan strategic moves in real time.

- **Medical diagnostic systems** : AI-assisted diagnostic systems choose the best treatment strategy for patients.

- **Financial sector** : AI systems optimize portfolios and calculate investment strategies.

12.8 Challenges of decision-making in AI agents

Despite progress, challenges in decision-making remain:

- **Complexity** : Many decision problems are computationally very complex.

- **Uncertainty** : Agents have to work with incomplete information.

- **Dynamic environments** : Real-time adjustments require flexible planning methods.

- **Explainability** : In safety-critical applications, decisions must be understandable.

12.9 Conclusion

Planning and decision-making are fundamental capabilities of intelligent agents. While classical planning methods work well in fixed environments, probabilistic models and learning-based methods are crucial for dealing with uncertainty and dynamic scenarios.

As machine learning and reinforcement learning advance, AI agents are becoming increasingly better at **developing optimal strategies autonomously** .

Chapter 13: Dealing with Uncertainty: Probabilistic Approaches

13.1 Introduction

In the real world, intelligent agents often operate in environments with incompleteness, uncertainty and variability. Whether in medicine, robotics or autonomous driving - agents often have to make decisions even though not all information is available to them.

Traditional rule-based or deterministic methods reach their limits in such scenarios. Therefore, probabilistic approaches are used to model uncertainties and make the best possible decision based on probabilities.

This chapter covers the most important probabilistic methods, including Bayesian networks, Markov models and Partially Observable Markov Decision Processes (POMDPs), and shows how AI agents can deal with uncertainties.

13.2 Why uncertainty is relevant in AI

An agent rarely has complete control over its environment. Various factors lead to it having to work with uncertainty:

- **Incomplete information** : A doctor does not have all the patient data and still needs to make a diagnosis.
- **Sensor noise** : A self-driving car can be affected by rain or snow.
- **Unpredictable changes** : A financial market can be affected by unpredictable events.
- **Dynamic environments** : A robot must adapt to moving obstacles.

An intelligent agent therefore needs methods to calculate probabilities and select the best action based on inaccurate or limited data.

13.3 Basics of Probability Theory in AI

Probability theory provides a mathematical basis for systematically modeling uncertainty.

Conditional **probability** is a central concept and is described by **Bayes' rule** :

$$P(A \mid B) = P(B \mid A) \cdot P(A) P(B) P(A \mid B) = \frac{P(B \mid A) \cdot P(A)}{P(B)} P(A \mid B) = P(B) P(B \mid A) \cdot P(A)$$

This rule describes how the probability of an event AAA, given an observation BBB, can be updated.

Example:

- A patient has a fever. How likely is it that he has the flu?
- Bayes' rule allows this probability to be calculated based on known probabilities.

13.4 Bayesian Networks: Modeling Uncertainty

A **Bayesian network** is a graphical model that represents probability distributions between variables. It consists of **nodes** (state variables) and **directed edges** (dependencies between variables).

13.4.1 Example of a Bayesian network

A simple medical diagnostic model may contain the following variables:

- *illness (H)*
- *Symptoms (S)*
- *test results (T)*

If a patient has a positive test result, the network can calculate the probability that he or she is actually sick.

13.4.2 Advantages of Bayesian networks

- Enable probabilistic inference based on known probabilities.
- Can take new information into account and update probabilities dynamically.
- Used in diagnostic systems, speech recognition and robotics.

13.5 Markov models: prediction of states over time

Markov models are probabilistic systems that predict future states based on the current state.

13.5.1 Markov chains

A Markov chain describes a sequence of states where the next state depends only on the current state and not on the past.

Example:

- A weather model that uses only the current state ("sunny" or "rainy") to predict the next state.

Markov chains are used in **speech recognition, financial models, and maintenance forecasting** .

13.5.2 Hidden Markov Models (HMMs)

A Hidden Markov Model (HMM) extends the concept by assuming hidden states that are indirectly observed.

Example:

- A speech processing system can only indirectly infer a speaker's intention from spoken language.

HMMs are used in **speech recognition, handwriting recognition and bioinformatics** .

13.6 Decision making under uncertainty: POMDPs

A Partially Observable Markov Decision Process (POMDP) is an extension of the classic Markov decision process in which the agent does not directly receive all information about the current state.

13.6.1 Components of a POMDP

A POMDP consists of:

- **States (SSS)** : The possible world configurations.
- **Actions (AAA)** : Decisions the agent can make.
- **Transition probabilities (TTT)** : Probability of changing from one state to another.
- **Observations (OOO)** : Limited information about the current state.
- **Reward function (RRR)** : Evaluates the quality of a decision.

13.6.2 Application of POMDPs

POMDPs are particularly useful for robotics, autonomous vehicles and assistance systems that need to deal with uncertainties in their environment.

Example:

- A self-driving car cannot perfectly observe other road users. A POMDP helps to make optimal decisions based on sensor information.

13.7 Monte Carlo methods for decision making

Monte Carlo methods are probabilistic approaches that optimize decisions through **simulations** .

13.7.1 Monte Carlo simulations

Monte Carlo simulations use random samples to calculate the expected value of different decisions.

Example:

- A financial system simulates thousands of market trends to calculate an optimal investment strategy.

Monte Carlo methods are used in **game AI, financial forecasting and risk analysis** .

13.8 Applications of probabilistic methods

Probabilistic approaches are indispensable in many areas of artificial intelligence:

- **Medical diagnostic systems** : Detect diseases using probabilistic models.
- **Autonomous vehicles** : Navigating uncertain environments using Bayesian filters.
- **Speech processing** : Recognizing spoken language despite noise or unclear pronunciation.
- **Finance** : Assess investment risks using Monte Carlo simulations.

13.9 Challenges of probabilistic methods

Despite their advantages, probabilistic methods also have challenges:

- **Computationally intensive** : Probability calculations often require high computing power.
- **Data dependence** : Quality of results depends on the quality of the training data.
- **Interpretability** : Some probabilistic models are difficult to understand or explain.

To address these challenges, hybrid approaches are being developed that combine probabilistic methods with **machine learning and heuristic techniques** .

13.10 Conclusion

Probabilistic methods are essential for intelligent agents that have to deal with uncertainty. Bayesian networks, Markov models and POMDPs enable agents to make informed decisions despite incomplete information.

In modern AI, probabilistic approaches are often combined with machine learning and deep learning to develop even more powerful systems.

Chapter 14: Reinforcement Learning – Reward-Based Learning

14.1 Introduction

Reinforcement Learning (RL) or reward-based learning is one of the most powerful methods in artificial intelligence. While classic search or planning algorithms find the best path through a known state space, an RL agent learns through interaction with its environment which actions are most beneficial in the long term.

This approach is particularly useful for problems where no direct model of the environment exists or where optimal strategies must be found through trial and error. RL is successfully used in **robotics, game AI, autonomous driving, and optimization processes** .

In this chapter, we look at the basic concepts of reinforcement learning, important algorithms such as Q-Learning and Deep Q-Networks (DQN), and applications and challenges of this approach.

14.2 Basics of Reinforcement Learning

In reinforcement learning, an agent acts in an environment and receives rewards or penalties for its actions. The goal is to develop a strategy (policy) that achieves the highest overall reward in the long term.

An RL process can be described by a Markov Decision Problem (MDM) Process , MDP), which consists of the following components:

- **States (SSS)** : The possible situations in which the agent finds itself.
- **Actions (AAA)** : The decisions the agent can make.
- **Transition model (PPP)** : Specifies the probability that an action leads from one state to another.
- **Reward Function (RRR)** : Defines the immediate reward for an action.
- **Discount Factor (γ\ gammay)** : Weights future rewards to encourage long-term strategies.

Example:

A self-driving car chooses between different driving speeds. If it drives too slowly, it loses time (negative reward); if it drives too fast, the risk of an accident increases (also negative reward). The goal is to learn a driving style that is safe and efficient.

14.3 Types of Reinforcement Learning

There are two main types of reinforcement learning:

14.3.1 Model-based RL

In this approach, the agent knows the probabilistic transitions between states and uses this knowledge to make decisions.

Example: A chess AI agent can anticipate all possible moves and calculate which move offers the best chance of winning.

14.3.2 Model-free RL

Here the agent learns **directly through interaction with the environment** without having a model of the environment.

Example: A robot tests different gripping techniques through trial and error until it finds an optimal method.

Model-free RL is particularly useful for **complex and dynamic environments** where the rules are unknown or difficult to model.

14.4 Value functions and strategies

Reinforcement learning algorithms use **value functions** to evaluate the quality of a state or action.

14.4.1 State-value function ($V(s)V(s)V(s)$)

Describes the expected future utility of a state sss if the agent pursues an optimal strategy.

$$V(s)=E[\sum t=0\infty \gamma\ tRt]V(s) = E \left[\sum\_{t=0}^{\{\ infty \}} \gamma^t R\_t \right]V(s)=E[t=0\sum\infty \gamma tRt$$

14.4.2 Action -value function ($Q(\ s,a\ )Q(\ s,a\ )Q(\ s,a\ )$)

Describes the expected future utility if the agent in state sss chooses action aaa and then acts optimally.

$$Q(\ s,a\ )=E[R+\ \gamma\ maxa\ 'Q\ (\ s\ ',a\ '\ )]Q(s, a) = E \left[R + \gamma \max\_{a'} Q(s', a') \right]Q(\ s,a\ )=E[R+\ \gamma\ a'maxQ\ (\ s',a\ ')]$$

The **Q-function** is the basis of many RL algorithms, especially the well-known **Q-learning** .

14.5 Important RL algorithms

There are various methods to solve RL problems. The most important algorithms are **Q-learning, deep Q-networks (DQN) and policy gradient methods.**

14.5.1 Q-Learning

Q-Learning is a model-free RL method that learns the optimal Q-value function step by step through trial-and-error .

$$Q(s,a) = Q(s,a) + \alpha [R + \gamma \max_{a'} Q(s', a') - Q(s, a)]$$

Here:

- α\ alpha α is the learning rate .
- γ\ gamma γ is the discount factor.
- RRR is the reward for the current action.

Q-learning works well for problems with small state spaces, but for complex environments, storing all possible states becomes impractical.

14.5.2 Deep Q-Networks (DQN)

DQN extends Q-learning by using deep neural networks to approximate the Q-function.

Instead of storing a table for all $Q(s,a)$ values, DQN uses a neural network that learns based on experience.

DQN was developed by DeepMind and has managed to beat human players in classic Atari games by simply learning through play.

14.5.3 Policy gradient methods

In contrast to Q-learning, which optimizes a value function, policy gradient algorithms directly learn a strategy $\pi(a \mid s)$ that specifies which action is best in which state.

A well-known algorithm is the REINFORCE algorithm, which optimizes a policy by maximizing rewards.

These methods are often used in robotics and autonomous systems because they can learn continuous actions.

14.6 Exploration vs. Exploitation

A central aspect of RL is the balancing act between exploration and exploitation:

- **Exploration** : The agent tries new actions to discover better strategies.
- **Exploitation** : The agent uses its previous knowledge to obtain maximum reward.

A common method to control this balance is the ε- greedy strategy, in which the agent performs a random action with probability ϵ to explore new possibilities.

14.7 Applications of Reinforcement Learning

RL is used in many real-world applications:

- **Autonomous vehicles** : Optimize their driving behavior through continuous learning from real and simulated environments.
- **Robotics** : Robots learn to move safely and efficiently through RL.
- **Game AI** : AlphaGo and AlphaZero use RL to outperform human players.
- **Financial markets** : Trading algorithms use RL to find optimal investment strategies.
- **Energy optimization** : Smart grids optimize energy consumption through RL.

14.8 Challenges of Reinforcement Learning

Although RL is powerful, there are several challenges:

- **Long training times** : Agents often need millions of iterations to learn optimal strategies.
- **High computational effort** : RL requires powerful hardware, especially for Deep RL.
- **Instability** : Small changes in the environment can drastically affect learned behavior.
- **Difficulty with complex actions** : RL algorithms often have problems with **continuous action spaces** , e.g. in real-world robotics.

Hybrid approaches that combine RL with **knowledge-based methods or probabilistic models** help to overcome some of these challenges.

14.9 Conclusion

Reinforcement learning is one of the most important techniques in modern AI. Through trial-and-error and reward mechanisms, agents learn to make optimal decisions.

With the advancement of deep RL and policy gradient techniques, RL is increasingly being used in real-world applications, from autonomous vehicles to industrial control systems.

Chapter 15: Multi-Agent Systems – Basics and Concepts

15.1 Introduction

In many real-world applications, intelligent systems do not operate in isolation, but in an environment with other agents. Multi-agent systems (MAS) consist of several autonomous agents that cooperate, compete, or act independently of each other.

These systems play a crucial role in areas such as swarm intelligence, robotics, networked systems and economic simulations. They are able to solve complex problems that a single agent could not handle.

In this chapter we look at the fundamentals, types of multi-agent systems, cooperation and competition concepts, and applications in modern artificial intelligence.

15.2 What are multi-agent systems?

A multi-agent system consists of several agents interacting in a common environment. Each agent has:

- **Autonomy** : He can make decisions independently.

- **Communication skills** : He can exchange information with other agents.

- **Cooperative or competitive behavior** : He can work together with others or act against them.

MAS are used to develop distributed , scalable and adaptable systems.

15.2.1 Examples of multi-agent environments

- **Autonomous vehicles** : Multiple self-driving cars communicate to optimize traffic flow.

- **Robot swarms** : Drones or robots coordinate to achieve a common goal.

- **Economic simulations** : Virtual markets in which agents make buying and selling decisions.

- **Game AI** : Computer game characters act as individual agents in a shared environment.

15.3 Types of Multi-Agent Systems

MAS can be divided into different categories depending on the degree of cooperation, control and objectives.

15.3.1 Cooperative Multi-Agent Systems

In cooperative systems, agents work **together** to achieve a common goal.

Examples:

- **Search and rescue drones** : Several drones are working in a coordinated manner to search for survivors.

- **Industrial manufacturing** : Robots share tasks to optimize production.

Advantages:

- Efficient problem solving through division of labor.

- Scalability through distributed decision making.

15.3.2 Competitive Multi-Agent Systems

In competitive MAS, agents compete **and** try to achieve their own goals.

Examples:

- **Stock trading** : Automated trading algorithms compete for the best time to buy.

- **Game AI** : Several agents fight for victory in a strategy game.

Advantages:

- Can simulate real-world markets and competitive situations.

- Promotes strategic decision making.

15.3.3 Hybrid multi-agent systems

Many real-world scenarios contain both cooperative and competitive elements.

Example:

- **Soccer AI Agents** : Players of one team cooperate while competing against another team.

15.4 Communication in Multi-Agent Systems

Agents need to communicate with each other to make effective decisions, using different protocols and languages.

15.4.1 Direct vs. indirect communication

- **Direct communication** : Agents exchange messages in a standardized format.

    o Example: Two autonomous vehicles coordinate a right-of-way rule.

- **Indirect communication (stigmergy)** : Agents interact via changes in the environment.

    o Example: Ants leave scent trails to mark the best path to a food source.

15.4.2 Agent Communication Languages (ACLs)

Standardized languages such as FIPA-ACL (Foundation for Intelligent Physical Agents - Agent Communication Language) enable structured agent communication.

This type of message can be interpreted by AI agents to make situation-dependent decisions.

15.5 Decision-making in multi-agent systems

Since multiple agents interact with different goals, they must use decision-making mechanisms.

15.5.1 Negotiation strategies

Agents negotiate to find compromises or share resources.

Example: Two autonomous vehicles negotiate who will enter a narrow street first.

15.5.2 Mechanism design and auction procedure

In economic scenarios, agents can use auctions to allocate resources efficiently.

Example: In cloud computing platforms, AI agents bid on computing capacity.

15.5.3 Game Theory in Multi-Agent Systems

Game theory concepts help to develop optimal strategies for agents that influence each other.

Example:

- **Prisoner's dilemma** : Two agents decide independently whether to cooperate or cheat.

Game theory is used in **traffic control, financial models and social networks** .

15.6 Learning in Multi-Agent Systems

Agents can improve their strategies through machine learning and reinforcement learning.

15.6.1 Multi-Agent Reinforcement Learning (MARL)

Agents learn through interaction with their environment and other agents.

Example:

- **Robot swarms learn how to cover an area efficiently.**
- **AI players learn to develop cooperative strategies.**

15.6.2 Swarm intelligence

In swarm intelligence systems, many agents follow simple rules, resulting in complex and efficient behaviors.

Examples:

- Flocks of birds optimize flight formations.
- Logistics systems adapt dynamically to changing demand.

15.7 Applications of Multi-Agent Systems

MAS are indispensable in many areas of modern AI:

- **Traffic management** : Autonomous vehicles communicate to avoid traffic jams.
- **Aerospace** : Satellite networks coordinate for earth observation.
- **Financial markets** : Trading agents optimize buying and selling strategies.
- **Industry 4.0** : Machines in a smart factory optimize production processes.
- **Crisis management** : Agent systems coordinate rescue operations in the event of disasters.

15.8 Challenges of Multi-Agent Systems

Although MAS are powerful, there are some challenges:

- **Scalability** : Many agents increase computational complexity.

- **Coordination** : Agents must resolve conflicts efficiently.

- **Communication costs** : Too many messages can slow down the system.

- **Security and trustworthiness** : In safety-critical applications, MAS must be robust.

To solve these problems, hybrid approaches are used that combine MAS with machine learning, probabilistic methods and rules.

15.9 Conclusion

Multi-agent systems are a central component of modern AI and enable complex problems to be solved through distributed, autonomous decision-making processes. They are used in robotics, financial markets, smart cities and game AI.

With the further development of reinforcement learning and swarm intelligence, MAS are becoming increasingly more powerful and flexible.

Chapter 16: Communication and Cooperation between Agents

16.1 Introduction

In a multi-agent system (MAS), communication is a key aspect for effective collaboration. Agents must exchange information in order to jointly solve problems, avoid conflicts or optimize strategies.

Communication can occur explicitly through message transmission or implicitly through changes in the environment. In this chapter, we examine how agents communicate with each other, which protocols and languages are used, and which mechanisms enable cooperation between agents.

16.2 Why is communication important?

Without communication, multi-agent systems would be severely limited. In cooperative scenarios, agents must share information to achieve common goals, while in competitive scenarios they often exchange strategic information.

16.2.1 Examples of agent-based communication

- **Autonomous vehicles** share real-time data on road conditions to avoid accidents.

- **Search and rescue robots** coordinate to search areas efficiently.

- **Smart grids** optimize energy consumption through the exchange of information between consumers and producers.

Communication can be organized differently depending on whether it is direct or indirect.

16.3 Types of communication between agents

16.3.1 Direct communication

Agents send explicit messages to other agents. This form of communication requires a **common language** and a defined **communication protocol** .

Example:

An autonomous vehicle tells another vehicle: "I am driving at 50 km/h towards the intersection, please give way."

Advantages:

- Enables precise coordination.
- Efficient when agents share information in a targeted manner.

Disadvantages:

- Requires synchronization between agents.
- Communication failures can lead to problems.

16.3.2 Indirect communication (stigmergy)

Agents communicate by changing their environment. This method is often used in **swarm intelligence systems** .

Example:

- **Ants leave pheromone trails** to mark the best path to a food source.
- **Robot vacuum cleaners recognize cleaned areas** and adjust their route accordingly.

Advantages:

- More robust against communication failures.
- Enables distributed, self-organizing systems.

Disadvantages:

- Lower precision and speed of information transfer.

16.4 Communication protocols in multi-agent systems

In order for agents to communicate effectively, they need a common protocol to structure their messages.

16.4.1 Agent Communication Language (ACL)

The **Agent Communication Language (ACL)** is a standard for exchanging messages between agents. A typical message might look like this:

ACLs enable structured, machine-readable messages.

16.4.2 Communication types in MAS

Agents can use different communication strategies:

- **Peer-to-peer (direct connection between two agents).**
- **Broadcasting (send message to all agents).**
- **Mediated Communication (A central intermediary coordinates messages).**

For example, in a **smart home system,** a central agent (e.g. a smart hub) could relay messages between sensors and devices.

16.5 Cooperation between agents

Cooperation occurs when agents work together to achieve a **common goal .**

16.5.1 Types of cooperation

1. **Explicit cooperation** : Agents share goals and actively work together.
   - o   Example: Two robots coordinate the lifting of a heavy object.
2. **Implicit cooperation** : Agents work independently, but their actions complement each other.
   - o   Example: A swarm of drones shares a surveillance task.

16.5.2 Mechanisms for cooperation

- **Task division:** Agents specialize in different subtasks.
- **Resource sharing:** Agents share data, energy or tools.
- **Consensus building:** Agents negotiate to reach a common decision.

Example:

- **Autonomous delivery drones** coordinate to optimize delivery routes.
- **Industry 4.0 robots** distribute production tasks dynamically.

16.6 Negotiation and conflict resolution in MAS

Not all agents have the same goals. In many cases they must **negotiate** to resolve conflicts.

16.6.1 Negotiation models

1. **Cooperative negotiation** : Agents look for a win-win solution.
   - o   Example: Two robots coordinate access to a limited power source.
2. **Competitive negotiation** : Agents compete for resources.

o   Example: Two sales agents bid for the best price.

16.6.2 Conflict resolution mechanisms

- **Auction process** : Resources are auctioned.

- **Mediators** : A central agent mediates between the parties.

- **Rule-based conflict resolution** : A set of rules decides on priorities.

Example:

- An air traffic system allocates landing rights based on a **priority rule** .

- Autonomous vehicles use **auctions** to agree on lanes.

16.7 Learning and adaptation in cooperative agent systems

Agents can learn to communicate and cooperate more effectively through machine learning and **reinforcement learning** .

16.7.1 Multi-Agent Reinforcement Learning (MARL)

Here, agents learn through **trial and error** how to best interact.

Example:

- **Football-playing AI agents** learn through RL to develop better team strategies.

- **Drones in a search and rescue team** learn how to cover areas efficiently.

16.7.2 Swarm intelligence in cooperative agent systems

Swarm-based systems use **decentralized decision-making** to solve complex problems.

Example:

- **Ant algorithms** help in **route planning** for delivery vehicles.

- **Bee-inspired algorithms** optimize **data traffic in networks** .

16.8 Applications of cooperative multi-agent systems

MAS with effective communication and cooperation are used in many areas:

- **Traffic control** : Vehicles coordinate to avoid traffic jams.

- **Logistics** : Warehouse robots distribute themselves dynamically to sort packages efficiently.

- **Game AI** : AI players develop team strategies in real time.

- **Smart Cities** : Intelligent agents optimize energy consumption and traffic flows.

- **Disaster management** : Drones and rescue teams coordinate search and relief operations.

16.9 Challenges in agent communication and cooperation

Although multi-agent systems offer great potential, there are challenges:

- **Communication costs** : Too many messages can overload the system.

- **Synchronization** : Delays in communication can lead to inefficient decisions.

- **Trustworthiness** : In safety-critical systems, messages must be verifiable.

- **Scalability** : Large MAS must be able to grow efficiently.

Solutions include hybrid communication models, machine learning for adaptive coordination, and decentralized decision-making mechanisms.

16.10 Conclusion

Communication and cooperation are essential components of intelligent multi-agent systems. They enable agents to solve problems together, share resources and adapt to dynamic environments.

With advances in reinforcement learning, swarm intelligence and probabilistic models, MAS are becoming more powerful and versatile.

Part III: Practical Development of AI Agents

Chapter 17: Approach to developing AI agents

17.1 Introduction

Developing an AI agent is a complex process that requires both technical and conceptual considerations. From defining the intended use to choosing suitable algorithms to implementation and optimization, developers have to make a series of decisions.

A well-thought-out development process helps to create efficient, robust and adaptable agents that work reliably in different environments. This chapter describes the most important phases of AI agent development, provides insights into best practices and highlights typical challenges.

17.2 Phases of developing an AI agent

The development of an AI agent takes place in several steps, ranging from planning to implementation to continuous improvement.

17.2.1 Phase 1: Problem definition and objective setting

Before an AI agent is developed, it must be clear what problem it should solve. This includes:

- **Goal of the agent:** What task should he take on?

- **Environment:** In what environment will the agent operate?

- **Degree of autonomy:** How independently should the agent be able to act?

- **Interaction:** Should the agent communicate with people or other agents?

Example:

An autonomous delivery robot needs clear goals: **Should it only transport packages or also detect and avoid obstacles?**

17.2.2 Phase 2: Choice of agent architecture

The architecture determines how the agent perceives its environment, makes decisions and performs actions. There are different architectures:

- **Reflex-based agents:** Make decisions based on direct inputs (e.g. thermostats).

- **Goal-oriented agents:** acting based on given goals.

- **Utility-based agents:** Calculate probabilities and optimal actions.

- **Learning agents:** Improve their behavior through machine learning.

Example:

An autonomous vehicle could be a combination of utility-based and learning agents to navigate optimally.

17.2.3 Phase 3: Selection of algorithms and methods

Depending on the architecture, suitable algorithms must be chosen.

- **Search algorithms:** For path planning (e.g. A* algorithm).

- **Optimization methods:** For decision making (e.g. genetic algorithms).

- **Machine learning:** For self-improving agents (e.g. reinforcement learning).

- **Probabilistic models:** For agents that need to deal with uncertainty (e.g. Bayesian networks).

Example:

A customer support chatbot requires natural language processing (NLP), while a chess AI agent uses minimax search algorithms.

17.2.4 Phase 4: Implementation and prototyping

After the theoretical planning, the actual implementation of the agent begins. Important aspects are:

- **Programming language:** Python is popular for AI development (e.g. with TensorFlow or PyTorch).

- **Frameworks and libraries:** OpenAI Gym for reinforcement learning, ROS for robotics.

- **Prototyping :** First simple versions of the agent to test functionality.

Best Practices:

- Agile methods such as **SCRUM** help to make iterative improvements.
- **Modular programming** facilitates later extensions.

17.2.5 Phase 5: Training and optimization

Learning agents need to be trained and optimized in an environment.

- **Supervised Learning:** Using labeled data for training.
- **Reinforcement Learning:** Agent learns through interaction with its environment.
- **Hyperparameter tuning:** Adjustment of learning rates, neuron layers or reward functions.

Example:

An AI agent for facial recognition is trained with millions of images to improve its accuracy.

17.2.6 Phase 6: Testing and validation

The agent must be thoroughly tested before actual use.

- **Unit tests:** checking individual functions.
- **Simulation testing:** Agent is tested in an artificial environment.
- **Real-world testing:** testing in real-world applications.

Example:

A self-driving car is first tested in a **virtual simulation** before it is allowed on the road.

17.2.7 Phase 7: Deployment and Monitoring

After successful testing, the agent is integrated into its real environment.

- **Deployment strategies:** cloud integration or local implementation.
- **Error monitoring:** Continuous monitoring to detect errors.
- **Feedback loops:** Use user feedback to improve the agent.

17.3 Tools and technologies for AI development

There are numerous tools that facilitate the development of AI agents.

17.3.1 Programming languages and frameworks

- **Python** : Most widely used for AI development.
- **R** : Statistical analysis and machine learning.
- **Java** : Often used in enterprise AI solutions.

Popular frameworks:

- **TensorFlow / PyTorch** : Deep Learning.

- **OpenAI Gym** : Reinforcement Learning.
- **ROS (Robot Operating System)** : Robotic Agents .

17.3.2 Development environments and simulation tools

- **Gazebo** : Simulation of robots.
- **Unity ML- Agents** : Training AI agents in virtual worlds.
- **SUMO** : Simulation for traffic control.

17.3.3 Hardware for AI agents

- **GPUs (NVIDIA Tesla, RTX 3090)** for neural networks.
- **Edge computing (NVIDIA Jetson , Raspberry Pi)** for mobile agents.

17.4 Challenges in the development of AI agents

Although AI agents are becoming more and more powerful, there are numerous challenges:

17.4.1 Data availability and quality

Many AI models are data-driven. Lack of or incorrect data can lead to poor results.

Solution: Use **data augmentation** and **synthetic data generation** .

17.4.2 Computing power and scalability

AI training often requires enormous computing resources.

Solution : Cloud computing (e.g. Google AI, AWS).

17.4.3 Transparency and explainability

Many AI agents, especially deep learning models, are difficult to interpret.

Solution: Use **Explainable AI (XAI)** for better traceability.

17.4.4 Safety and Ethics

AI agents must act safely and fairly.

Solution: Compliance with **ethical AI guidelines** , continuous security audits.

17.5 Conclusion

Developing AI agents is a multi-step process that requires clear planning, appropriate algorithms and continuous optimization. From defining the problem to implementation and monitoring, each stage must be carefully thought out.

With the right tools, a structured approach and continuous improvement, powerful agents can be developed that create real added value in a wide range of applications - from robotics to finance.

Chapter 18: Defining Requirements and Setting Goals

18.1 Introduction

The successful development of an AI agent begins with a clear definition of the requirements and goals. Without a thorough planning phase, there is a risk that the agent will not function optimally or will not deliver the desired results. The precise definition of the requirements influences all subsequent development phases, from the choice of algorithms to implementation and optimization.

This chapter explains how requirements for an AI agent can be systematically recorded and specified. This not only covers functional aspects such as the tasks of the agent, but also non-functional requirements such as security, scalability and ethical considerations. It also highlights how clear objectives enable the subsequent evaluation of an agent's performance.

18.2 Identification of the problem

Before the technical implementation can begin, the problem must be clearly understood. The key question is: What specific problem should the AI agent solve? The analysis begins with examining the current challenges in the respective domain and a precise definition of expectations.

For example, if an AI agent is to be used in the field of logistics, the problem could be inefficient delivery processes or delays in package delivery. In a medical scenario, AI could help support diagnosis or detect anomalies in large amounts of data.

An important part of defining the problem is analyzing existing solutions. It should be checked whether similar systems already exist and whether their approaches can be adopted or improved. It helps to involve various stakeholders - such as customers, developers and experts - in the planning early on in order to get a complete picture of the requirements.

18.3 Definition of functional requirements

Functional requirements describe the specific tasks that the AI agent should perform. These are the core functions of the agent and its behavior in different situations.

For example, an autonomous delivery robot would need to be able to correctly process delivery addresses, detect obstacles, calculate optimal routes and coordinate with other road users. A chatbot, on the other hand, needs mechanisms for speech recognition, understanding user requests and generating meaningful answers.

These requirements need to be formulated as precisely as possible. Instead of a vague description such as "The agent should answer customer queries", a more detailed requirement would be useful: "The agent should be able to analyze customer queries, retrieve relevant information from a knowledge base and generate an answer with at least 85% accuracy."

It is helpful to divide the functional requirements into scenarios or use cases. This allows you to systematically check whether the agent works reliably in different situations.

18.4 Non-functional requirements

In addition to the functional aspects, there are a number of non-functional requirements that go beyond the technical implementation. These include performance, security, scalability and ethical aspects.

The performance requirements concern aspects such as reaction times, accuracy and efficiency of the agent. An AI system that has to act in real time - such as an autonomous vehicle - requires extremely low latency and fast calculations. A system that processes large amounts of data, on the other hand, should have optimized memory management and efficient algorithms.

Another key point is reliability. The AI agent must also react appropriately in difficult or unforeseen situations. For example, a medical expert system should have a high level of error tolerance and ensure that incorrect decisions are minimized.

Security aspects also play a major role. An AI agent that works with sensitive data must be protected from external attacks. In the financial sector or when dealing with personal data, it must be ensured that all processing steps comply with statutory data protection guidelines.

Finally, ethical considerations cannot be neglected. AI agents that make decisions about people must work fairly, transparently and comprehensibly. Discriminatory or unfair decisions due to distortions in the training data must be excluded.

18.5 Goal definition for the AI agent

A well-defined AI agent needs clear goals. These goals must not only reflect the expected functionality, but also be measurable and verifiable. The so-called SMART method helps to formulate realistic and verifiable goals:

- **Specific :** The goal should be clearly and precisely formulated.
- **Measurable :** The agent's success must be quantifiable .
- **Achievable :** The goal should be realistic and achievable with the available resources .
- **Relevant:** The goal should be relevant in the context of the project.
- **Time-bound :** There should be a clear deadline for achieving the goal.

An example of a SMART objective would be: "The AI agent should be able to answer customer inquiries correctly in 95% of cases and reduce the average processing time from 30 seconds to 5 seconds. This goal should be achieved within the next six months."

By clearly defining the goals, not only can the progress of the project be better monitored, but the agent's success can also be objectively evaluated later.

18.6 Stakeholder involvement and requirements analysis

The development of an AI agent often involves a large number of participants, including developers, subject matter experts and end users. It is therefore essential to involve all relevant stakeholders in the requirements process at an early stage.

An interdisciplinary team helps to take different perspectives into account. The IT department could formulate technical requirements, while end users express practical expectations regarding usability. Decision makers in companies could, in turn, pay attention to cost-effectiveness and efficiency.

Workshops, interviews and feedback sessions help to get a comprehensive picture of expectations. In agile development processes, this requirements analysis is regularly reviewed and adapted to new findings.

18.7 Challenges in requirements definition

Precisely formulating requirements can be difficult, especially when the project involves new technologies or complex environments. Common challenges include unclear objectives, conflicting expectations among stakeholders, or changing conditions.

Another difficulty is the uncertainty about the performance of AI. Especially with learning agents, it is often difficult to predict how well they will behave in real scenarios. This is where prototyping and regular test phases help to iteratively refine the requirements.

Ethical issues also pose a challenge. In many cases, it must be ensured that the agent does not adopt biases from training data or violate regulatory requirements. Transparency in decision-making and explainable AI models are crucial factors here.

18.8 Conclusion

Clearly defining requirements and goals is a fundamental step in the development of an AI agent. Functional and non-functional requirements must be considered equally in order to develop a powerful, safe and ethical agent.

Careful requirements analysis can help avoid later implementation problems. Close collaboration with all stakeholders and iterative adaptation of requirements ensure that the AI agent is optimally tailored to the needs of its users.

Chapter 19: Modeling and Design of the Agent

19.1 Introduction

After defining the requirements and goals, the actual design of the AI agent begins. In this phase, the system model is created, which serves as a blueprint for later implementation. Well-thought-out modeling ensures that the agent can act efficiently, scalably and flexibly.

The design of an AI agent includes several aspects: the choice of agent architecture, the definition of perception and action, the determination of decision strategies and the specification of communication mechanisms. Depending on the application, different modeling approaches can be chosen, from rule-based systems to learning agents with neural networks.

This chapter describes how to structure and design an AI agent, which models are suitable for different scenarios, and how concepts such as modularity and interoperability can improve the efficiency of the agent.

19.2 Architecture of the Agent

The architecture of an AI agent determines how it processes information, makes decisions and interacts with its environment. There are various basic approaches that can make sense depending on the application.

19.2.1 Reflex-based architecture

Reflex-based agents work according to the "if-then" principle. They react immediately to perceptions without relying on extensive internal modeling of their environment. This architecture is suitable for simple applications with clearly defined rules.

An example of a reflex-based agent is an **automatic door opener** that detects movement and then opens the door. Many control systems that respond to simple sensor values work in a similar way.

19.2.2 Goal-oriented architecture

Goal-oriented agents have an internal model of their goal and plan their actions to achieve this goal in the best possible way. They evaluate possible actions based on their effect on the desired outcome and choose the one with the highest chance of success.

A navigation system is a typical example of a goal-oriented agent. It analyzes different routes and chooses the fastest or safest connection based on real-time data.

19.2.3 Benefit-based architecture

Utility-based agents go beyond purely goal-oriented systems by focusing not only on goal achievement but also on optimizing intermediate goals. They evaluate their actions based on a utility function that takes into account various criteria such as efficiency, safety or resource utilization.

A self-driving car is an example of a utility-based agent. It not only makes decisions based on whether it reaches its destination, but also takes into account factors such as energy consumption, traffic flow, and safety.

19.2.4 Learning Architecture

Learning agents continuously improve their behavior by interacting with their environment. They use machine learning to recognize patterns, optimize strategies, and adapt to changing conditions.

For example, an AI-based stock trading agent can use reinforcement learning to learn which buying and selling strategies are most profitable in the long term. Such systems are particularly powerful, but require an extensive training phase and corresponding computing resources.

19.3 Perception and Environment

In order for an AI agent to act sensibly, it must perceive its environment. Perception occurs via sensors or data interfaces that provide the agent with information.

19.3.1 Sensors and data sources

The type of perception depends on the environment in which the agent operates. In robotics, agents use cameras, LIDAR or ultrasonic sensors, while software agents use databases, APIs or sensor networks to obtain information.

A voice assistant processes audio data via microphones, while a financial AI agent analyzes market data. In both cases, the data needs to be processed and interpreted before it can be used for decision-making.

19.3.2 Modeling the environment

An agent must understand how its environment changes. To do this, various environmental models are used:

- **Static environments** do not change and the agent can create its plan based on predictable conditions.

- **Dynamic environments** require continuous adaptation of the agent as environmental conditions are constantly changing.

For example, an autonomous delivery robot operates in a dynamic environment as pedestrians, vehicles and weather conditions vary. A chess AI agent, on the other hand, operates in a static environment where all possible moves are known in advance.

19.4 Decision-making and action

The decision strategy of an AI agent determines how it chooses between different options for action.

19.4.1 Rule-based decision-making

Some agents use fixed decision rules based on logical if-then conditions. This method is particularly useful when the problem is well-structured and predictable.

For example, a chatbot could have a fixed rule: "If the customer asks about opening hours, answer with the saved times."

19.4.2 Decision trees and heuristics

Decision trees are used for more complex decision-making processes. These visualize possible courses of action and evaluate them based on probabilities or heuristics.

For example, an automated diagnostic system could use a decision tree to determine the most likely disease based on symptoms.

19.4.3 Reinforcement Learning and Neural Networks

Learning algorithms are used for particularly complex and dynamic environments. Reinforcement Learning (RL) enables agents to develop optimal strategies through trial and error.

An autonomous vehicle could learn through RL when to accelerate or brake in order to drive both safely and efficiently.

19.5 Architectural design and modularity

A well-designed AI agent should be modular to facilitate future extensions or adaptations.

By separating the agent into perception, decision and action modules, it can be flexibly adapted. For example, a robot could be equipped with new sensors without having to change its entire control system.

Another important principle is interoperability. Many AI systems need to communicate with other programs or physical devices. Open interfaces and standardized protocols help to integrate the agent into existing systems.

19.6 Challenges in modeling an AI agent

Developing an agent brings with it various challenges. A central difficulty is the balance between autonomy and controllability. While a highly autonomous agent reacts flexibly to its environment, this can also lead to unpredictable decisions.

Another problem is computational complexity. Training often requires enormous computing capacity, especially for agents that can learn. Optimized algorithms or distributed computation models can help here.

The explainability of decisions is also a critical point. With complex neural networks, it is often difficult to understand why an agent made a certain decision. To ensure trust in AI systems, Explainable AI (XAI) methods are increasingly being used.

19.7 Conclusion

Modeling and designing an AI agent are crucial steps that determine the performance and efficiency of the system. From choosing the right architecture to designing the decision-making processes, many factors must be taken into account.

Careful planning can ensure that the agent not only performs its tasks efficiently, but also remains scalable, adaptable and understandable.

Chapter 20: Selection of suitable algorithms and data structures

20.1 Introduction

The performance of an AI agent depends largely on the algorithms and data structures used. They determine how efficiently the agent processes data, makes decisions and interacts with its environment. While simple agents can get by with rule-based procedures, complex systems require advanced search, optimization and learning algorithms.

The choice of algorithms and data structures depends heavily on the type of task. For example, a route planning agent needs efficient search algorithms, while a learning agent can use optimized neural networks. At the same time, data must be stored and processed in such a way that it can be accessed quickly and resource consumption is minimized.

This chapter introduces the most important algorithms and data structures for AI agents, analyzes their advantages and disadvantages, and explains their application in different scenarios.

20.2 Criteria for the selection of algorithms

Not every algorithm is suitable for every task. The selection is based on various criteria, including:

- **Runtime complexity** : How efficiently does the algorithm work as the amount of data grows?

- **Memory requirements** : How much memory is needed?

- **Accuracy** : How precise are the results of the algorithm?

- **Scalability** : Can the algorithm be adapted to larger data sets or more complex environments?

- **Robustness** : How well does the algorithm perform with incomplete or noisy data?

For example, a learning agent operating in a highly dynamic environment requires an algorithm that can react quickly to new data, while a chess AI agent primarily needs efficient search strategies.

20.3 Algorithms for search and decision processes

Many AI agents need to search through information or make optimal decisions in a complex state space. There are various proven algorithms for this.

20.3.1 Uninformed search algorithms

These algorithms systematically explore the state space without using additional information about the problem.

- **Breadth-first search (BFS)** : systematically searches all possibilities in increasing depth. It guarantees the shortest solution, but is memory-intensive.

- **Depth-first search (DFS)** : Delves deep into the search space before exploring alternative paths. It requires less memory but can be inefficient if it gets into long irrelevant paths.

Both methods are suitable for problems with manageable complexity or for scenarios in which it must be ensured that a solution is found.

20.3.2 Informed search algorithms

These algorithms use heuristics to make the search more efficient.

- *A-Algorithm* *: Combines the actual cost of a path with a heuristic to find the optimal solution as quickly as possible. Often used in navigation and planning applications.

- **Greedy Best-First Search** : Always chooses the most promising path based on a heuristic. Is faster, but can deliver suboptimal solutions.

Informed search algorithms are particularly useful for route planning, robotics and game AI because they enable targeted and rapid problem solving.

20.3.3 Optimization algorithms

Optimization methods are used for problems where an optimal solution must be found among many possibilities.

- **Genetic algorithms (GA)** : Simulate natural evolution through selection, mutation and recombination to gradually find better solutions. They are used for complex optimization problems such as machine scheduling or neural network optimization.

- **Simulated Annealing** : Uses a temperature-controlled strategy to not only refine the best known solution, but also allow random jumps that can find a better solution.

These algorithms are particularly suitable for optimization problems with many variables or uncertainties.

20.4 Machine Learning Algorithms

Learning agents require algorithms that can recognize patterns and make predictions from experience and data.

20.4.1 Supervised Learning

In supervised learning, algorithms are trained with already labeled data.

- **Linear Regression** : Calculates predictions based on a linear function. Useful for simple forecasting problems.

- **Decision trees** : Break down the data step by step into decision rules. Particularly useful for classification problems.

- **Neural networks** : Used for complex pattern recognition, especially in image and speech processing.

These methods are suitable for **speech recognition, image processing or predictive models** .

20.4.2 Unsupervised Learning

Here, patterns and structures are recognized in unlabeled data.

- **K -Means Clustering** : Divides data into clusters based on similarities. Used for customer segmentation or anomaly detection .

- **Principal Component Analysis (PCA)** : Reduces the number of variables by extracting the most important features.

These algorithms are helpful when the agent is supposed to recognize unknown structures independently.

20.4.3 Reinforcement Learning

In **reinforcement learning (RL),** the agent learns through trial and error.

- **Q-Learning** : Stores values for states and actions to learn the best strategy.

- **Deep Q-Networks (DQN)** : Combine Q-Learning with neural networks to operate in complex environments.

These methods are crucial for **autonomous systems, game AI and robotics** .

20.5 Important data structures for AI agents

In addition to the algorithms, the data structures used also influence the efficiency of an AI agent.

- **Graphs** : Used for search and planning problems. For example, the A* algorithm uses graphs for pathfinding.

- **Hash tables** : Provide quick access to stored information, for example in game AI.

- **Queues** : Important structure for algorithms such as breadth-first search or for event processing in multi-agent systems.

- **Heaps/Priority Queues** : Used in A* and Dijkstra algorithms to always make the next best decision efficiently.

Depending on the application, the agent must be designed so that its data can be processed and stored efficiently.

20.6 Challenges in algorithm and data structure selection

Choosing the right algorithms and data structures brings with it some challenges.

Firstly, an algorithm that works well in a simulation may be inefficient in the real world because it cannot handle uncertainty or unexpected changes. In addition, sophisticated algorithms can require large amounts of computing power, which is particularly problematic for mobile or embedded systems.

Another challenge is generality vs. specificity. While specialized algorithms are often more efficient, general methods can be adapted more flexibly. The choice must therefore be made carefully in order to find an optimal compromise.

20.7 Conclusion

The selection of suitable algorithms and data structures is a crucial factor for the performance of an AI agent. Search algorithms, machine learning and optimization techniques help to make intelligent decisions, while efficient data structures optimize processing speed.

Chapter 21: Implementation – Programming a Simple Agent

21.1 Introduction

After the theoretical planning, the practical step of implementation follows. In this phase, the agent is actually programmed, tested and optimized. The choice of programming language and development environment plays a central role. Python has established itself as the preferred language for developing AI agents because it offers a variety of libraries for machine learning, search algorithms and optimization.

This chapter walks through the process of programming a simple agent. It implements a basic reflex-based agent that makes decisions in an environment. This example provides a practical understanding of the concepts of agent perception, decision making, and action.

21.2 Selection of the development environment

Choosing the right environment makes implementing and testing the agent much easier. For simple AI agents, Python is particularly suitable due to its large number of libraries. A typical environment includes:

- **Python (3.x)** as a programming language
- **Jupyter Notebook or an IDE (e.g. PyCharm , VS Code)** for development
- **Libraries such as NumPy , OpenAI Gym and TensorFlow** , if machine learning is used

Once the environment is set up, implementation can begin.

21.3 Basic structure of a simple reflex-based agent

A reflex-based agent makes decisions based on the direct perception of its environment, without pursuing a long-term strategy. It is suitable for applications in which simple rules are sufficient to make meaningful decisions.

As an example, a virtual vacuum cleaner agent is programmed. It moves in a 2D environment and uses sensor data to decide whether it should clean the floor or move in another direction.

21.3.1 Definition of the environment

First, the agent's environment must be modeled. It consists of a grid field in which the vacuum cleaner can move. Some fields are dirty, others are clean.

The environment is represented as a grid model with randomly placed dirt fields. The vacuum cleaner can move around in it and check whether its current field needs to be cleaned.

21.3.2 Implementation of the agent

Now the reflex-based agent is programmed. It first checks whether the current location is dirty. If so, it cleans it. If not, it randomly moves in a new direction.

Each turn, the agent checks whether the current field is dirty and then decides whether to clean or move.

21.3.3 Execution of the simulation

Finally, the simulation is started. The agent acts in a predefined number of cycles and tries to clean the grid field.

This program simulates the functioning of a simple reflex-based agent. At each step, the grid shows the current state of the environment, including the position of the agent and the remaining dirt spots.

21.4 Extension of the agent

The simple reflex-based agent can be further improved. One possibility is to introduce a goal-oriented agent that remembers which fields have already been cleaned to avoid unnecessary movements.

A learning agent could be optimized using reinforcement learning to learn more efficient cleaning strategies. In this case, it could, for example, determine that it makes more sense to move in a certain direction rather than moving randomly.

21.5 Challenges in implementing an agent

While simple agents are relatively easy to program, more complex systems require sophisticated modeling and optimization. A key challenge is the efficiency of decision making. A reflex-based agent often makes suboptimal decisions because it does not consider long-term consequences.

Another problem is dealing with uncertainty. Many real-world environments provide incomplete or noisy data, making decision-making difficult. This is where probabilistic models or machine learning help to develop more robust agents.

Computing resources also play a role. A simple agent like the vacuum cleaner presented above can run on almost any hardware. Complex learning agents, on the other hand, often require powerful GPUs or cloud infrastructures.

21.6 Conclusion

Implementing an AI agent starts with a clear architecture and a suitable programming language. Reflex-based agents are easy to implement, but offer limited decision-making capabilities. By using more intelligent decision-making mechanisms or machine learning, agents can be made significantly more powerful.

Chapter 22: Testing and Validating Agent Behavior

22.1 Introduction

The development of an AI agent does not end with implementation. Before it can be deployed in a real environment, it must be thoroughly tested and validated. This ensures that the agent works as intended, makes robust decisions and operates reliably even under unexpected conditions.

Testing AI agents is particularly challenging because their behavior is often not fully predictable. While classic software tests rely on predefined inputs and expected outputs, AI agents must deal with dynamic and changing environments. This chapter presents best practices for debugging, performance evaluation, and optimization of an AI agent.

22.2 Objectives of testing and validation

Testing an AI agent has several goals:

- **Functional correctness:** The agent must perform its tasks correctly.
- **Efficiency:** Response times and resource consumption should be optimized.
- **Robustness:** The agent must react sensibly even under disturbances or incomplete data.
- **Scalability:** Performance should not degrade drastically as complexity increases.
- **Security:** The agent must not cause critical errors that could endanger its environment.

There are specific testing procedures for each of these areas, which are explained below.

22.3 Test strategies for AI agents

Since AI agents do not just execute static code but react to their environment, they require a combination of classic software testing and special AI-specific testing methods.

22.3.1 Unit tests for individual components

Even if an agent acts autonomously, it consists of different modules that can be tested individually. These include:

- **Perception tests:** Checks whether sensor data is processed correctly.
- **Decision testing:** Checks whether the agent makes the right decision in a given situation.
- **Movement tests (for physical agents):** Validates whether the agent moves correctly or performs manipulative tasks.

Unit tests help to detect errors early and ensure that individual modules of the agent function correctly.

22.3.2 Simulation tests in artificial environments

Because AI agents often operate in dynamic and unpredictable environments, they are often first tested in **simulated test environments** .

- **OpenAI Gym** is a platform that provides standardized test environments for reinforcement learning agents.
- **Gazebo** is used to simulate robots in 3D worlds.
- **Unity ML- Agents** enables testing of agents in a game-like environment.

A simulation helps to identify potential weaknesses before the agent is transferred to a real environment.

22.3.3 Testing with real data and hardware

Once the agent performs satisfactorily in a simulation, its behavior must be verified in a real environment.

- **Physical agents (e.g. robots):** Tests under real conditions check whether the agent can cope with unexpected obstacles.
- **Data-driven agents (e.g. chatbots):** Test with real user queries to ensure that the agent provides meaningful answers.

An example of a real-world test would be an autonomous vehicle that is first tested in a controlled environment, such as a proving ground, before being deployed on the road.

22.4 Evaluation methods for agent performance

Evaluating an AI agent requires quantitative and qualitative methods.

22.4.1 Metrics for measuring performance

- **Accuracy :** Percentage of correct decisions .
- **Reaction time:** How quickly does the agent make decisions?

- **Efficiency:** How many resources (computing power, energy) does the agent consume?

- **Error rate:** How often does the agent make wrong decisions?

- **Success rate:** How often does the agent achieve its defined goal?

An example of performance evaluation of a navigation agent could be:

$$\text{Durchschnittliche Zeit zur Zielerreichung} = \frac{\sum \text{Zeit aller Durchläufe}}{\text{Anzahl der Testläufe}}$$

Depending on the application, it may be useful to combine several metrics to obtain a holistic assessment.

22.5 Error detection and debugging

Misconduct of an AI agent can have various causes:

1. **Faulty data processing:** Sensors provide incorrect or incomplete values.

2. **Wrong decision logic:** The agent prioritizes suboptimal actions.

3. **Overtraining or bias:** The agent has become too focused on certain patterns and generalizes poorly.

4. **Instability:** Learning agents may experience unpredictable fluctuations in behavior.

The following techniques can be used to identify errors:

- **Logging :** Logs the agent's decisions to identify patterns in misbehavior.

- **Visual debugging tools:** Especially important for robotics or game AI to analyze why an agent makes certain decisions.

- **A/B testing :** Comparing different versions of the agent to see which one works better.

A practical example of debugging is analyzing the decision-making of a chatbot. If it gives inappropriate answers in certain situations, an analysis of the training data can show whether faulty or unbalanced data sets are influencing the behavior.

22.6 Optimization of agent behavior

After identifying errors and vulnerabilities, the agent can be improved.

- **Hyperparameter tuning:** If the agent uses machine learning, adjusting parameters such as learning rate or network size can improve performance.

- **Algorithmic adjustments:** If a decision algorithm is too slow or inefficient, a faster procedure can be implemented.

- **Data improvement:** If the agent performs poorly, more or better training data can be collected.

An iterative approach is crucial here: **test, analyze, optimize and test again.**

22.7 Conclusion

Testing and validating an AI agent is an essential step to ensure that it works correctly, efficiently and reliably. A combination of unit tests, simulations and real-world tests helps to detect errors early.

The agent is evaluated based on clearly defined metrics such as accuracy, efficiency and error rate. If problems occur, debugging techniques and optimization measures can be used to improve behavior.

Chapter 23: Training and Learning – Developing a Learning Agent

23.1 Introduction

While simple agents work rule-based and make their decisions based on predefined rules, learning agents are able to improve their strategies through experience. They adapt to new situations and optimize their behavior based on feedback from their environment.

The development of a learning agent requires the selection of suitable learning methods, training algorithms and data sources. Various techniques are used, including supervised and unsupervised learning as well as reinforcement learning. This chapter describes the basics of the training process, the selection of suitable learning algorithms and the practical implementation of a learning agent.

23.2 Fundamentals of Machine Learning for Agents

A learning agent is based on machine learning, a method in which systems recognize patterns from data and use them to make predictions or decisions. There are three main types of learning:

Supervised Learning

In supervised learning, a model is trained with labeled data. Each input is associated with an expected output. The model learns by adjusting its parameters to minimize the error rate.

Example:

A chatbot that analyzes customer messages can use training data to learn whether a request should be classified as "place an order" or "request support."

Unsupervised Learning

The agent recognizes patterns in data without being given correct answers in advance.

Example:

A recommender system groups customers based on purchasing behavior to create personalized recommendations.

Reinforcement Learning (RL)

In reinforcement learning, the agent learns by interacting with its environment. It receives rewards for good decisions and punishments for bad ones.

Example:

A self-driving car can learn through RL to develop optimal driving strategies by reaching its destination safely while obeying traffic rules.

23.3 Choosing the right learning algorithm

The choice of learning algorithm depends on the type of problem.

- **Neural networks** : Particularly useful for complex pattern recognition in image and speech recognition.
- **Decision trees** : Good for logical decisions, for example in expert systems.
- **Q-Learning (Reinforcement Learning)** : Useful for agents that need to develop long-term strategies.
- **Deep Q-Networks (DQN)** : Combination of reinforcement learning and neural networks for highly complex environments.

A learning agent for financial forecasting might use a neural network, while an autonomous robot is more likely to require an RL-based system.

23.4 Implementation of a learning agent with reinforcement learning

In the following, a simple learning agent is programmed using reinforcement learning. It should learn to move in a simulated environment and receive rewards for reaching a goal.

23.4.1 Installation of the required libraries

First, some libraries need to be installed. OpenAI Gym provides an environment for RL experiments, while NumPy and TensorFlow are used for computations.

```
pip install numpy gym tensorflow keras
```

23.4.2 Creating the environment

The environment simulates a simple grid field in which the agent can move. The goal is to reach a certain position in as few steps as possible.

```
import numpy as np

import gym

import random


# Vicinity initialize

env = gym.make ("FrozenLake-v1", is_slippery =False) # 4x4 grid world

state_size = env.observation _space.n

action_size = env.action _space.n
```

This environment represents a 4x4 grid in which the agent must avoid obstacles and reach the goal.

23.4.3 Implementation of a Q-Learning Agent

Q-learning is a reinforcement learning method in which an agent uses a **Q-table** to make optimal decisions.

```
# Q- table initialize

q_table = np.zeros (( state_size , action_size ))


# learning parameters

learning_rate = 0.1

discount_factor = 0.99

exploration_rate = 1.0 # Starts with high exploration

exploration_decay = 0.995

min_exploration_rate = 0.01


# Training

episodes = 1000


for episode in range(episodes):

state = env.reset ()[0]
```

```
done = False

while not done:
if random.uniform (0, 1) < exploration_rate :
action = env.action _space.sample () # Random action
else:
        action = np.argmax ( q_table [ state ]) # Best known action


    new_state , reward, done, _, _ = env.step (action)

    # Q-value update according to the Bellman equation
    q_table [ state, action] = q_table [state, action] + learning_rate * \
(reward + discount_factor * np.max ( q_table [ new_state ]) - q_table [ state , action])

state = new_state

# Exploration step by step reduce
  exploration_rate = max( min_exploration_rate , exploration_rate * exploration_decay )
```

23.4.4 Testing the trained agent

After training, the agent can be tested to see if it has learned to reach the goal efficiently.

```
state = env.reset ()[0]
done = False

while not done:
   action = np.argmax ( q_table [ state ]) # Select best known action
   state, reward, done, _, _ = env.step (action)
   env.render ()
```

If the training was successful, the agent should find the optimal path to the goal in most cases.

23.5 Challenges in training AI agents

The development of a learning agent involves several challenges:

1. **Exploration vs. exploitation:** The agent must find a balance between exploring new strategies and using already learned optimal solutions.

2. **Overtraining:** If the agent is too specialized in a particular environment, it may perform worse in other scenarios.

3. **Long training times:** Reinforcement learning can be very computationally intensive, especially for complex problems with many states.

4. **Instability of the learning process:** Especially in neural networks, learning can be unstable if the parameters are poorly chosen.

To solve these problems, methods such as **experience replay** or **adaptive learning rates can** be used.

23.6 Conclusion

A learning agent offers enormous advantages because it can adapt to new conditions. Reinforcement learning is a particularly powerful technique for training agents in dynamic environments.

The implementation of a simple RL agent shows how an agent can learn through trial and error. With more advanced methods such as neural networks or deep Q-networks, even more complex applications can be realized.

Chapter 24: Optimizing and Improving Agent Performance

24.1 Introduction

After implementing and training an AI agent, the optimization phase follows to further improve its performance. An agent that works well in a controlled environment may encounter unexpected challenges in real-world scenarios. Targeted optimization helps make it faster, more robust and more efficient.

Optimizing an AI agent involves several aspects: improving learning algorithms, reducing computation times, using resources efficiently, and adapting to dynamic environments. This chapter covers the most important methods for improving performance and shows how modern techniques such as hyperparameter tuning, parallelization, and transfer learning can be used.

24.2 Identification of optimization potential

Before improvements are made, it is necessary to analyze where there is potential for optimization. There are several questions to ask:

- **Is the agent's decision making too slow?** → Optimization of algorithms and calculations required.

- **Does the agent make suboptimal decisions?** → Improvement of the learning strategy or training data necessary.

- **Does the agent require too many resources?** → Reducing memory consumption or parallelization makes sense.

- **Is the agent behaving unstably or unreliably?** → Stabilizing the learning process through regular adaptations.

A systematic performance analysis provides the basis for targeted improvements.

24.3 Optimization of learning algorithms

24.3.1 Hyperparameter tuning

Many AI algorithms have parameters that affect their ability to learn. These parameters are called **hyperparameters** and must be carefully chosen for optimal performance.

Typical hyperparameters are:

- **Learning rate (α\ alpha α)** : Determines how quickly the agent adapts. Too high values lead to unstable behavior, too low to slow learning.

- **Discount factor (γ\ gammaγ)** : Specifies how much future rewards are weighted.

- **Exploration rate ($\square$\ epsilon $\square$)** : Controls the ratio between exploring new strategies and using known solutions.

An example of hyperparameter tuning in Python with GridSearch :

```python
from sklearn.model _selection import ParameterGrid


param_grid = {

" learning_rate ": [0.01, 0.05, 0.1, 0.5] ,

" discount _factor ": [0.9, 0.95, 0.99],

" exploration_rate ": [1.0, 0.5, 0.1 ]

}


best_score = float('-inf')
```

```
best_params = {}


for params in ParameterGrid ( param_grid ):
    score = train_agent (** params ) # A function that trains the agent with these parameters
    if score > best_score :
        best_score = score
        best_params = params


print( " Best Parameter combination :", best_params )
```

Automated hyperparameter tuning saves time and significantly improves learning performance.

24.3.2 Adjustment of the reward function

In many cases, the reward function directly influences how the agent learns. A poorly chosen reward function can cause the agent to develop undesirable behavior.

Example:

- A self-driving car might be rewarded for reaching a destination, but if it is not penalized for hitting other vehicles, it might learn risky driving.

- An improved reward function takes into account not only reaching the destination, but also safe and energy-efficient driving.

24.4 Improving efficiency and computing power

24.4.1 Parallelization and distributed learning

If an agent requires many iterations, training can take a long time. One way to speed things up is through parallelization, where multiple copies of the agent are trained simultaneously.

An example of parallel training with multiprocessing in Python:

```
import multiprocessing as mp


def train_agent (seed):
env = create_environment (seed)
agent = ReinforcementAgent (env)
    agent.train ()
```

```
return agent.evaluate ()


if __name__ == "__main__":

with mp.Pool (processes=4) as pool: # Uses 4 CPU cores

results = pool.map ( train_agent , range(4))

    print ( "Average performance:", sum ( results ) / len ( results ))
```

Distributed learning allows an agent to be trained faster by having multiple instances explore different learning paths simultaneously.

24.4.2 Reducing storage and computing load

Especially with deep neural networks, the calculations can be very resource-intensive. Opportunities for optimization are:

- **Weight quantization :** Reducing the precision of model parameters to save memory space.

- **Pruning :** Removing unnecessary neural connections from neural networks to speed up computations.

- **Memory optimization through mini-batches:** Instead of processing all the data at once, the training is divided into smaller sections.

An example of pruning a neural network with TensorFlow :

```
import tensorflow_model_optimization as tfmot


model = create_neural_network ( )
pruned_model = tfmot.sparsity .keras.prune_low_magnitude (model)


pruned_ model.compile (optimizer=" adam ", loss=" categorical_crossentropy ", metrics=["accuracy"])
```

Through such optimizations, an AI agent can work significantly faster and more resource-efficiently.

24.5 Adaptation of the agent to dynamic environments

An important aspect of optimization is the ability to react to new situations. Reinforcement learning agents in particular can have difficulties when the environment changes.

24.5.1 Transfer Learning

Instead of training an agent from scratch, transfer learning can be used to apply previously learned knowledge to new problems.

Example:

- An agent that has been trained on a small playing field can transfer its knowledge to a larger playing field through transfer learning without having to learn completely from scratch.

In neural networks, transfer learning is often used with pre-trained models:

```
from tensorflow.keras .applications import VGG16


base_model = VGG16(weights=" imagenet ", include_top =False)
new_model = add_custom_layers ( base_model )
new_  model.compile  (optimizer="  adam  ",  loss=" categorical_crossentropy ",
metrics=["accuracy"])
```

This technique saves enormous computing time and improves the generalization ability of the agent.

24.5.2 Dynamic adjustment of the exploration rate

An agent must continuously learn in a changing environment. An adaptive exploration strategy can help:

- **High exploration at the beginning:** The agent explores different options.
- **Exploration reduction during training:** Once an optimal strategy has been found, the agent focuses on proven actions.
- **Dynamic adaptation to new environments:** If the environment changes, the agent should explore more intensively again.

An example of an adaptive exploration rate:

```
def adaptive_exploration_rate ( timestep , min_rate =0.01, decay_factor =0.001):
return max( min_rate , np.exp (- decay_factor * timestep))
```

This technique allows the agent to adapt more flexibly to new environments.

24.6 Conclusion

Optimizing an AI agent is a continuous process that can be improved through targeted hyperparameter tuning, parallelization, efficient computational methods, and adaptations to dynamic environments.

The balance between performance and resource consumption is particularly important in order to develop an efficient and scalable agent. Methods such as transfer learning and adaptive exploration rates help to improve the generalization ability.

Chapter 25: Case Study – Developing a Complete AI Agent

25.1 Introduction

After the theoretical foundations and optimization methods, a case study on the development of a complete AI agent follows. This chapter shows the step-by-step implementation of a practical project - from problem definition to implementation to training and optimization of the agent.

The case study covers the development of an autonomous delivery robot that transports packages from a warehouse to different destinations in a simulated environment. The agent uses reinforcement learning to learn optimal routes, avoid obstacles and minimize delivery times.

25.2 Problem definition and requirements

The delivery robot should perform the following tasks:

- Collect packages from a central warehouse and transport them to various delivery points.
- Finding your way in an environment with roads, intersections and obstacles.
- Choose an efficient route to minimize delivery time.
- Avoid collisions with other objects.
- React flexibly to changes in the environment (e.g. roadblocks).

These requirements specify that the agent will use a goal-oriented architecture with reinforcement learning.

25.3 Modeling the environment

25.3.1 Simulated urban environment

The environment is modeled as a grid network in which streets and buildings are represented. The agent moves in this grid and can pick up or deliver packages at certain points.

An example of a 5x5 grid environment:

```
nginx

S . . X G
. X . . .
. . . X .
. . X . .
L . . . .
```

- **S:** starting position of the robot
- **L:** warehouse
- **G:** Destination of delivery
- **X:** Obstacles (e.g. buildings)
- **.** : Walkable streets

25.4 Implementation of the agent

25.4.1 Creating the environment with OpenAI Gym

First, an OpenAI Gym environment is defined that represents the simulation area:

```python
import gym
import numpy as np
from gym import spaces

class DeliveryEnv ( gym.Env ):
def __init__( self, grid_size =5):
    super( DeliveryEnv , self).__init__()
    self.grid _size = grid_size
    self.state = (0, 0) # Starting position of the robot
    self.package_location = (4, 0)
    self.delivery _point = (0, 4)

    self.action _space = spaces.Discrete (4) # 4 possible movements: Up, Down, Left, Right
    self.observation _space = spaces.Tuple (( spaces.Discrete ( grid_size ), spaces.Discrete
( grid_size )))

def step( self, action):
x, y = self.state

if action == 0 and x > 0: # High
x -= 1
```

```
        elif action == 1 and x < self.grid _size - 1: # Down
x += 1
        elif action == 2 and y > 0: # Left
y -= 1
        elif action == 3 and y < self.grid _size - 1: # Right
y += 1

        self.state = (x, y)

        reward = - 1 # Small penalty for each movement
        done = False

if self.state == self.package_location :
        reward += 10 # Reward for picking up the package

    if self.state == self.delivery_point :
        reward += 50 # Higher reward for successful delivery
        done = True

return self.state , reward, done, {}

    def reset ( self ):
        self.state = (0, 0) # Reset to the start position
        return self.state
```

This environment ensures that the agent receives meaningful rewards: movement costs energy, picking up a package brings a moderate reward, and successful delivery is heavily rewarded.

25.4.2 Implementation of a Reinforcement Learning Agent

To train the agent we use **Q-Learning** , a simple method of reinforcement learning.

```
import random

class QLearningAgent :
def __ init __ ( self, env, learning_rate =0.1, discount_factor =0.99, exploration_rate =1.0,
exploration_decay =0.995):
    self.env = env
    self.q _table = np.zeros (( env.grid_size , env.grid_size , env.action_space.n ))
    self.learning _rate = learning_rate
    self.discount _factor = discount_factor
    self.exploration_rate = exploration_rate
    self.exploration _decay = exploration_decay

def choose_action ( self, state) :
if random.uniform (0, 1) < self.exploration_rate :
return self.env.action _space.sample () # Random action
```

```
else:
x, y = state
        return np.argmax ( self.q_table [x, y]) # Best known action

   def update_q_ table ( self, state, action, reward, next_state ):
x, y = state
    nx , ny = next_state
    best_next_action = np.argmax ( self.q_table [ nx , ny ])

    self.q _table [x, y, action] = (1 - self.learning_rate ) * self.q_table [x, y, action] + \
                    self.learning _rate * (reward + self.discount_factor * self.q_table [ nx ,
ny , best_next_action ])

def train( self, episodes=1000):
for episode in range(episodes):
state = self.env.reset ()
done = False

while not done:
action = self.choose _action (state)
        next_state , reward, done, _ = self.env.step (action)
        self.update _q_table (state, action, reward, next_state )
state = next_state

    self.exploration_rate * = self.exploration_decay # Reducing exploration
```

25.5 Training and optimization of the agent

The agent is trained using the Q-learning method. After a few thousand episodes, it should have learned to find the fastest route to the destination.

```
env = DeliveryEnv ( grid_size =5)

agent = QLearningAgent (env)


agent.train ( episodes =5000)
```

After training, the agent can be tested:

```
state = env.reset ()

done = False


while not done:

action = agent.choose_action (state )

state, _, done, _ = env.step (action)
```

```
print ( f"Agent moves to { state }")
```

With sufficient training, the agent should be able to choose the most efficient route and deliver packages quickly.

25.6 Challenges and optimization opportunities

The development of such an agent brings challenges:

- **Slow learning:** In more complex environments, training takes a long time. This could be accelerated by Deep Q-Networks (DQN).

- **Exploration vs. exploitation:** A high exploration value causes the agent to try many random actions, while a value that is too low prevents it from finding new solutions. Adaptive ε- greedy strategies help here.

- **Dynamic environment:** If roads are suddenly closed or delivery destinations change, an adaptive model with transfer learning could be used.

25.7 Conclusion

This case study shows how a complete AI agent can be developed, trained and optimized from scratch. The combination of environmental modeling, reinforcement learning and strategic optimization creates an agent that can adapt to a dynamic environment.

Part IV: Technical Tools and Frameworks

Chapter 26: Programming languages and development environments for AI agents

26.1 Introduction

Choosing the right programming language and development environment is a crucial factor for the successful development of an AI agent. Different languages and tools offer specific advantages that have different effects depending on the type of agent and its requirements.

While **Python** is the most used language for AI development due to its extensive libraries and simple syntax, there are also other powerful options such as **Java, C++, R and Julia** . In addition, specialized development environments and frameworks such as **TensorFlow** , **PyTorch** , **OpenAI Gym or ROS (Robot Operating System) make it easier** to implement and test AI agents.

This chapter provides an overview of the most suitable programming languages and development tools and explains their strengths, weaknesses and typical areas of application.

26.2 Programming languages for AI agents

The choice of programming language depends on various factors:

- **Performance:** How efficiently does the language process large amounts of data?
- **Flexibility:** How easy is it to implement different AI models?
- **Libraries and community support:** Is there enough support for machine learning and AI?
- **Application area:** Is the agent being developed for web applications, embedded systems or high-performance computing?

26.2.1 Python – The standard for AI development

Why Python?

- Extensive AI and ML libraries: TensorFlow , PyTorch , scikit-learn , OpenAI Gym
- Simple syntax and readability
- Large community and support
- Ideal for rapid prototyping and research

Areas of application:

- Machine Learning and Deep Learning
- Reinforcement Learning
- data analysis and NLP (Natural Language Processing)
- Simulations and test environments for AI agents

26.2.2 Java – Scalability and Enterprise Solutions

Why Java?

- Platform independent and stable
- Good for large, scalable AI systems
- Machine learning libraries (e.g. Deeplearning4j)

Areas of application:

- AI agents for companies and financial markets
- web and cloud applications
- embedded systems

26.2.3 C++ – Speed and Efficiency

Why C++?

- High computing power and efficiency
- Good for robotics and real-time AI
- Used in autonomous vehicles, high-performance computing and game AI

Areas of application:

- Autonomous Systems and Robotics
- High-performance real-time AI (e.g. for trading systems)
- Simulations and games (e.g. AI for NPCs)

26.2.4 R – Specialized in data analysis and statistics

Why R?

- Strong for statistical analyses and AI models
- libraries like Caret, XGBoost and randomForest
- Good for predictive analytics and financial AI

Areas of application:

- Data Analysis for AI Agents
- Predictive Models in the Financial Industry
- Processing large amounts of data for machine learning

26.2.5 Julia – Modern language for numerical calculations

Why Julia?

- Faster than Python, but similarly simple
- Good support for machine learning and AI
- Libraries like Flux.jl for deep learning

Areas of application:

- high-performance AI models
- Scientific simulations
- Reinforcement Learning

26.3 Development environments for AI agents

26.3.1 TensorFlow & PyTorch – Deep Learning for AI Agents

These frameworks are the leading libraries for neural networks and deep learning.

- **TensorFlow** : Scalable and efficient, especially for production AI

- **PyTorch** : More flexible and better for research and experiments

26.3.2 OpenAI Gym – Simulation environment for reinforcement learning

OpenAI Gym provides ready-made environments for testing RL agents, including CartPole , FrozenLake , and Atari games.

26.3.3 ROS (Robot Operating System) – Standard for Robotics AI

For AI agents in robotics, ROS (Robot Operating System) is the most important development platform.

- Control and communication between sensors and actuators
- Integration with Reinforcement Learning for Autonomous Robots

26.4 Conclusion

The choice of programming language and development environment depends heavily on the type of AI agent. While Python is ideal for most AI and ML applications, C++ and Java offer advantages for high-performance and enterprise solutions. Julia and R are useful for data-driven analytics and statistical AI models.

Specialized frameworks such as **TensorFlow , PyTorch , OpenAI Gym and ROS** make developing, training and testing intelligent agents much easier.

Chapter 27: Important Libraries for Machine Learning and AI

27.1 Introduction

Developing AI agents requires powerful libraries that efficiently perform complex calculations and facilitate training and optimization. In recent years, various machine learning and AI libraries have emerged that significantly accelerate the development process.

These libraries offer ready-made algorithms for neural networks, reinforcement learning, computer vision and natural language processing (NLP). Different tools are used depending on the agent's area of application. While TensorFlow and PyTorch dominate for neural networks, OpenAI Gym and Stable-Baselines3 are essential for reinforcement learning.

This chapter provides an overview of the most important AI and ML libraries, their features and typical use cases.

27.2 Machine Learning Libraries

27.2.1 Scikit-learn – Standard library for classical machine learning

Scikit-learn is one of the most widely used machine learning libraries and contains a variety of algorithms for regression, classification, clustering and dimensionality reduction.

Main functions:

- Implementation of Decision Trees , Support Vector Machines (SVMs) and Random Forests
- feature engineering and preprocessing
- clustering algorithms (e.g. K-Means, DBSCAN)
- Pipeline mechanisms for automating model training

Areas of application:

- Classification and Regression for AI Agents
- prediction models
- data analysis and feature engineering

27.2.2 XGBoost – Gradient Boosting for High-Performance Models

XGBoost (Extreme Gradient Boosting) is a powerful machine learning library that is often used in competitions and production systems.

Main functions:

- Extremely fast training times
- Boosting methods for improving weak models
- Very suitable for tabular data

Areas of application:

- financial forecasts and market analyses
- Automated decision-making
- AI agents that work on structured data

27.3 Libraries for Deep Learning

27.3.1 TensorFlow – Scalable AI Development

TensorFlow , developed by Google, is one of the leading libraries for deep learning and is used in production and research.

Main functions:

- Supports deep neural networks (CNNs, RNNs, Transformers)
- Can scale to GPUs and TPUs
- Includes Keras, a high-level API for easier model development

Areas of application:

- image processing (computer vision)

- natural language processing (NLP)
- Scalable AI agents in the cloud

27.3.2 PyTorch – Flexible Deep Learning for Research

PyTorch , developed by Facebook, is preferred for its dynamic computational graphs and ease of use. It is especially popular for research and experimentation with neural networks.

Main functions:

- Easy debugging through dynamic graphs
- Strong support for reinforcement learning
- Native GPU acceleration

Areas of application:

- Reinforcement Learning
- research on neural networks
- real-time AI agents

27.4 Libraries for Reinforcement Learning

27.4.1 OpenAI Gym – Standard for RL environments

OpenAI Gym provides simulated environments for reinforcement learning and is often used for training AI agents in games, robotics, and autonomous driving.

Areas of application:

- simulations for autonomous driving
- game AI (e.g. Atari Games)
- robot control

27.4.2 Stable Baselines3 – RL algorithms for rapid development

Stable-Baselines3 is a collection of reinforcement learning algorithms that build on OpenAI Gym and provide standardized interfaces.

Areas of application:

- Development of RL agents for industrial applications
- optimization of decision-making processes
- simulation of complex environments

27.5 Conclusion

Choosing the right library depends on the requirements of the AI agent. Scikit-learn and XGBoost are ideal for classic ML tasks, while TensorFlow and PyTorch enable deep learning. OpenAI Gym and Stable-Baselines3 are essential for reinforcement learning agents.

These tools can be used to develop, train and optimize powerful AI agents.

Chapter 28: Simulation and Test Environments for Agents

28.1 Introduction

Before AI agents are deployed in real-world applications, they must be tested and optimized in a controlled environment. Simulation environments allow developers to analyze an agent's behavior without taking risks or incurring high costs.

Whether it is an autonomous robot, a self-driving vehicle, or a trading AI, a good test environment helps to detect errors early and improve the system. This chapter introduces various simulation and test environments for AI agents, describes their use cases, and explains methods for using them effectively.

28.2 Why are simulations important?

The use of simulations offers several advantages:

- **Safety:** Agents can be trained in virtual environments without causing real damage or costs.

- **Scalability:** Millions of tests can be performed in a short period of time, which would not be practical in the real world.

- **Flexibility:** Simulation environments enable testing under different conditions, including extreme scenarios.

- **Reproducibility:** Errors can be specifically analyzed and corrected because tests can be carried out repeatedly under identical conditions.

A classic example is the training of autonomous vehicles in simulation software before they are sent onto real roads.

28.3 Simulation environments for reinforcement learning

28.3.1 OpenAI Gym – The standard for RL agents

OpenAI Gym is the most widely used simulation platform for reinforcement learning (RL). It offers a variety of pre-built test environments, including:

- **CartPole :** A balancing problem in which an agent must stabilize a pole.

- **MountainCar :** A car that has to climb a hill with limited power.

- **Atari Games:** A collection of classic video games for developing game AI.

28.3.2 Stable-Baselines3 – Ready-made RL algorithms for fast training

Stable-Baselines3 is an extension of OpenAI Gym and provides pre-built reinforcement learning algorithms, including:

- Deep Q-Networks (DQN)
- Proximal Policy Optimization (PPO)
- Soft Actor- Critic (SAC)

28.4 Simulation environments for robotics

28.4.1 ROS (Robot Operating System) – Standard for robotics simulations

ROS is an open source platform for robotics development and enables the simulation of physical robot systems in virtual environments.

Main functions:

- communication between sensors and actuators
- Controlling Robots via Reinforcement Learning
- Integration with hardware for real-world testing

Areas of application:

- simulation and control of robots
- development of autonomous vehicles
- Machine Control in Industry

An example of a ROS-controlled simulation is the control of an autonomous TurtleBot robot in a virtual environment.

28.4.2 Gazebo – Highly realistic 3D simulation for robotics

Gazebo is a powerful simulation platform for physics-based robot simulations. It is often combined with ROS to model realistic environments.

Main functions:

- physics simulations (e.g. collisions, gravity)
- 3D rendering for visual testing
- Integration with reinforcement learning models

Gazebo is ideal for **autonomous robots, drones and industrial automation** .

28.5 Simulation environments for autonomous vehicles

28.5.1 CARLA – Simulation environment for autonomous driving

CARLA is an open-source platform for training self-driving cars. It offers realistic 3D environments with different traffic conditions.

Main functions:

- real-time simulation of driving behavior
- Reinforcement Learning for Driving Strategies
- Integration with sensors (LIDAR, cameras, GPS)

28.6 Simulation environments for game AI

28.6.1 Unity ML- Agents – AI training in virtual game worlds

Unity ML- Agents is a powerful framework for AI agents in games and simulations. It combines deep learning with 3D simulations.

Main functions:

- Reinforcement Learning in Virtual Game Worlds
- Control of NPCs (Non-Player Characters)
- simulation of autonomous systems

Areas of application:

- Training of Game AI
- development of virtual assistants
- AI optimization for complex decision-making processes

28.7 Methods for evaluating simulation agents

Once the AI agent has been tested in a simulation environment, its performance must be measured. There are various evaluation methods for this:

1. **Success rate:** How often does the agent reach the goal?
2. **Efficiency:** How quickly does the agent solve a task?
3. **Error rate:** How often does the agent make suboptimal decisions?
4. **Exploration behavior:** Does the agent use the environment efficiently or does it stick to known strategies?

28.8 Conclusion

Simulation and test environments are essential for developing safe and powerful AI agents. While OpenAI Gym and Stable-Baselines3 are ideal for reinforcement learning, Gazebo and CARLA enable realistic robotics and vehicle simulations.

By using these environments, developers can test agents under realistic conditions, minimize errors, and develop optimal strategies before deploying them in the real world.

Chapter 29: Frameworks for Multi-Agent Systems and Agent-Based Modeling

29.1 Introduction

Multi-agent systems (MAS) are a central component of modern AI applications. They consist of several autonomous agents that interact to achieve a common goal. Such systems are used in robotics, traffic control, financial markets, logistics and simulation of social systems.

The development of MAS requires specialized frameworks that facilitate communication, decision making, and interaction between agents. This chapter provides an overview of the most important frameworks for multi-agent systems (MAS) and agent-based modeling.

29.2 Basics of Multi-Agent Systems

A multi-agent system (MAS) consists of several autonomous units operating in a common environment. Each agent has specific capabilities, goals and its own strategy for solving problems.

Typical characteristics of MAS

- **Autonomy:** Each agent makes its own decisions.
- **Communication:** Agents exchange information.
- **Cooperation or competition:** Agents can cooperate or compete.
- **Adaptivity:** MAS adapt to changing conditions.

An **autonomous traffic management system** would be an example of a MAS:

- Self-driving cars communicate with each other to avoid traffic jams.
- Traffic lights dynamically adapt their switching to the traffic flow.

Specialized MAS frameworks are used to develop such systems.

29.3 Frameworks for Multi - Agent Systems

29.3.1 JADE – Java Agent DEvelopment Framework

JADE is one of the best-known frameworks for developing distributed multi-agent systems. It is based on Java and supports FIPA-ACL (Agent Communication Language) to standardize communication between agents.

Main functions:

- Providing an agent platform with distributed agents
- Message-based communication between agents
- Integration with other systems via REST APIs and web services
- Support for ontology-based knowledge

Areas of application:

- Industrial automation (e.g. intelligent production lines)
- traffic management
- Distributed AI Agents in Smart Cities

29.3.2 SPADE – Agent framework for Python

SPADE is a Python-based multi-agent framework that is characterized by easy implementation and modern network communication.

Main functions:

- Communication via the XMPP protocol (ideal for cloud and IoT agents)
- Event-driven agent architecture
- Interaction with other AI services, e.g. for reinforcement learning

Areas of application:

- IoT agents in smart homes
- Agent-based web services
- Distributed AI systems

29.3.3 Mesa – Agent-based modeling in Python

Mesa is a powerful Python framework for agent-based simulation, particularly suitable for socioeconomic modeling, epidemiology, and environmental research.

Main functions:

- modeling of social interactions
- support for geographic data analysis
- visualization of simulation results

Areas of application:

- Epidemiological models (e.g. simulation of virus spread)
- simulation of social networks
- Agent-based economic models

29.4 Specialized frameworks for agent-based simulations

In addition to the general MAS frameworks, there are specialized frameworks for agent-based modeling (ABM). These are often used for research, market analysis and traffic control.

29.4.1 NetLogo – simulation environment for agent-based models

NetLogo is a graphical simulation platform that allows simulating thousands of agents simultaneously.

Main functions:

- Easy to learn thanks to visual programming
- simulation of complex social systems
- Interactive adjustment of parameters during simulation

Areas of application:

- social sciences (e.g. migration patterns)
- economic simulations
- traffic control

29.5 Comparison of the most important MAS frameworks

framework	programming language	special features	areas of application
JADE	Java	Industry standard, FIPA ACL communication	Industrial automation, traffic control
SPADE	python	XMPP communication for cloud agents	IoT agents, web services
Mesa	python	Agent-based simulations with visualization	social sciences, economics
NetLogo	own language	Easy to use, ideal for non-technical users	Simulations in Research & Education

29.6 Conclusion

Choosing the right MAS framework depends on the type of system, the required scalability and the programming language.

- **JADE and SPADE** are ideal for **distributed multi-agent systems** in industry and IoT.
- **Mesa and NetLogo** are suitable for **agent-based simulations in research and science** .

The use of MAS frameworks accelerates the development of intelligent, distributed systems and enables realistic simulations of autonomous agents in complex environments.

Chapter 30: Development Tools: IDEs, Debugging and Version Control

30.1 Introduction

Developing a powerful AI agent requires not only a suitable programming language and libraries, but also an efficient development environment. Modern development tools make it easier to write, debug, test and manage code.

This chapter introduces the most important integrated development environments (IDEs), debugging tools, and version control systems that are specifically suited for AI and machine learning.

30.2 Integrated Development Environments (IDEs) for AI Development

An IDE (Integrated Development Environment) provides a comprehensive environment with a code editor, debugging tools, package management and version control.

30.2.1 PyCharm – The best IDE for Python-based AI development

PyCharm is one of the most powerful IDEs for Python and is particularly well suited for machine learning and AI agents.

Main functions:

- Intelligent code completion and error detection
- Integrated debugging tools for Python scripts
- Seamless integration with TensorFlow , PyTorch and scikit-learn
- Jupyter Notebook support for interactive work

Areas of application:

- development of machine learning models
- Implementing AI Agents in Python
- Automated Debugging

Example: Setting up PyCharm for AI development

1. Create a new project and choose a **virtual environment (venv)** .
2. Install libraries directly in PyCharm :

```
pip install tensorflow numpy gym
```

3. Use **breakpoints and variable inspection** in the debugger to find errors.

30.2.2 VS Code – Lightweight and flexible IDE for AI projects

Visual Studio Code (VS Code) is a lightweight but powerful IDE that extensibility and cloud integration.

Main functions:

- Extensions for AI development (TensorFlow , Jupyter , PyTorch)
- Debugger for Python, Java, C++ and more
- Git integration for version control
- Cloud connectivity for remote training of AI models

Areas of application:

- Development of cloud-based AI agents
- Combined AI development with Python, JavaScript and C++
- Working with Jupyter Notebooks and Docker

30.2.3 Jupyter Notebook – Interactive development environment for data science

Jupyter Notebook is a standard tool for interactive programming in AI and data science projects.

Main functions:

- Live coding and visualization of data
- Easy experimentation with AI models
- Integration with TensorFlow , PyTorch and scikit-learn
- Integration of Markdown for documentation

Areas of application:

- Experimental AI Development
- visualization of training progress
- creation of interactive research reports

30.3 Debugging techniques for AI agents

Debugging is particularly challenging in machine learning models and reinforcement learning agents, as complex models often do not provide clear error messages.

30.3.1 Classic debugging techniques

- Set breakpoints: Use debugger in PyCharm or VS Code .
- logging : Output important variable values.
- Writing unit tests: Test individual functions separately.

30.3.2 Debugging for neural networks

- Checking the input data: Are all features scaled correctly?
- Visualization of training processes: Use Matplotlib or TensorBoard .
- Review of the model architecture: Is the network too big or too small?

Areas of application:
- Debugging **reinforcement learning agents**
- optimization of **neural networks**
- Error Analysis in **Data Processing Pipelines**

30.4 Version control with Git for AI projects

Version control is essential for collaborative AI development, especially for larger projects with multiple team members.

30.4.1 Using Git and GitHub for AI agents

Why Git ?
- Traceable changes to the code.
- Collaborative work in teams.
- Backup and rollback function for code versions.

30.4.2 Using DVC (Data Version Control) for AI projects

DVC is an extension of Git designed specifically for data science and AI models.

Why DVC?
- Manages large data sets and model versions.
- Reproducibility of AI experiments.
- Integrates seamlessly with Git .

Areas of application:
- version control for machine learning models
- Comparison of model variants and hyperparameters
- Collaborative AI development in teams

30.5 Conclusion

Modern development tools enable efficient, error-free and collaborative development of AI agents.

- **PyCharm , VS Code and Jupyter Notebook** offer powerful development environments.

- **Logging , debugging and TensorBoard** facilitate error analysis.
- **Git and DVC** ensure structured and traceable version control.

The combination of these tools significantly accelerates the development process and ensures reliable and scalable AI agents.

Chapter 31: Platforms for chatbots and voice assistants

31.1 Introduction

Chatbots and voice assistants are now an integral part of many applications - from customer support and e-commerce to intelligent personal assistants. Thanks to advanced natural language processing (NLP), modern systems can conduct human-like conversations and process requests efficiently.

The development of such systems requires powerful platforms and frameworks that support speech processing, dialogue management and integrations with external services. This chapter introduces the most important platforms for chatbots and voice assistants, their functions, areas of application and implementation options.

31.2 Basics of chatbots and voice assistants

Chatbots are programs that conduct text-based conversations with users, while voice assistants additionally integrate speech processing and voice output.

31.2.1 Main components of chatbots

- **Natural Language Understanding (NLU):** Understands the meaning of user input.
- **Dialogue management:** Decides how the bot responds to a request.
- **Integration with databases & APIs:** Retrieves information from external systems.
- **Response generation:** Creates an appropriate text or speech output.

For example, an e-commerce chatbot could inform customers about product availability or accept an order.

31.3 Platforms for chatbots

31.3.1 Dialogflow (Google) – AI-powered NLP platform

Dialogflow is a powerful platform from Google Cloud that provides natural language processing for chatbots and voice assistants.

Main functions:

- Natural language understanding with Google NLP technology.
- Support for multiple languages and dialects.

- Easy integration with Google Assistant , WhatsApp, Facebook Messenger and websites.
- Machine learning for continuous conversation improvement.

Example: Creating a simple intent in Dialogflow

1. Create a project in **Dialogflow CX or ES** .
2. Define an **intent** for a greeting:
   - User: "Hello!"
   - Bot: "Hello! How can I help?"
3. Connect the chatbot to a **webhook** to retrieve external data.

Areas of application:

- customer support chatbots for businesses
- voice assistants for Google Assistant
- Automated booking systems

31.3.2 IBM Watson Assistant – Enterprise solution for intelligent bots

IBM Watson Assistant is a cloud-based AI platform that is particularly suitable for enterprise applications.

Main functions:

- AI-supported speech recognition and text processing.
- Extensible conversation flows and multi-turn dialogs.
- Integration with CRM systems such as Salesforce and Zendesk .
- On- premise hosting for data protection-sensitive applications.

Areas of application:

- Enterprise customer support (banks, insurance companies, authorities)
- Intelligent chatbots for websites and call centers
- Voice bots for speech recognition systems

31.3.3 Rasa – Open source platform for context-based chatbots

Rasa is one of the most popular open source platforms for companies that want complete control over their chatbots.

Main functions:

- Advanced AI-supported dialogue guidance with machine learning.
- Can be hosted locally or in the cloud (no vendor lock-in).

- Supports multiple conversation flows with reminders and slots.
- API integration for custom backend functionality.

Areas of application:

- AI-supported support bots with complex dialogues
- Personalized Conversational AI for Business
- Self- hosted bots with complete data control

31.4 Platforms for voice assistants

31.4.1 Amazon Lex – NLP backend for Alexa and chatbots

Amazon Lex is the platform behind Alexa and enables developers to create their own voice assistants and chatbots.

Main functions:

- Automatic speech recognition (ASR) and NLP.
- Seamless integration with AWS Lambda and Amazon Polly for speech output.
- Easy connection with Alexa Skills, Slack, Facebook Messenger.

Example: AWS Lex for a simple voice assistant

1. Create an **intent** in the AWS console.
2. Train the voice assistant with example sentences.
3. Connect Lex to an AWS Lambda script to process requests.

Areas of application:

- Amazon Alexa skills
- Voice-based AI agents for call centers
- Automatic voice dialogue systems (IVR)

31.4.2 Microsoft Azure Bot Service – Chatbots with AI integration

Microsoft Bot Framework provides a cloud solution for interactive bots that can be extended with Azure Cognitive Services .

Main functions:

- Integration with Microsoft Teams, Skype and Slack.
- Connect to AI-powered speech processing with Azure Speech.
- Integration into corporate CRM and ERP systems.

Areas of application:

- Intelligent Helpdesk Bots for Enterprises
- Voice-controlled Office 365 integrations

- Call center automation with AI support

31.5 Conclusion

There are a variety of platforms for developing chatbots and voice assistants, each with different strengths depending on the use case:

- Dialogflow and Amazon Lex offer cloud-based NLP solutions with easy API integration.
- IBM Watson Assistant is suitable for enterprise applications with AI-powered analytics.
- Rasa is ideal for developers who need an open source solution with full control.

Voice assistants and chatbots are becoming increasingly powerful and offer companies enormous automation and personalization opportunities.

Chapter 32: Cloud Services and AI APIs (pre-built AI functions)

32.1 Introduction

Developing a powerful AI agent often requires a variety of machine learning, image recognition, natural language processing, and data analytics capabilities. Instead of implementing these capabilities from scratch, major cloud providers offer ready-made AI APIs that handle these tasks.

Cloud AI services enable scalable, powerful, and cost-effective use of AI without the need to manage your own hardware or complex ML models. This chapter introduces the most important cloud platforms and AI APIs that can be used for AI agents.

32.2 Benefits of Cloud AI Services

The use of AI APIs and cloud services offers several advantages:

- **Fast integration** : AI functions can be integrated directly into applications via REST APIs.
- **Scalability** : Cloud services adapt dynamically to needs.
- **Cost efficiency** : There is no need to train your own AI models or provide hardware infrastructure.
- **Current models** : AI APIs use the latest algorithms and are regularly updated.
- **Flexibility** : Support for different programming languages and platforms.

These services are ideal for chatbots, voice assistants, image recognition, machine translation, and predictive analytics.

32.3 Overview of the most important cloud AI services

32.3.1 Google Cloud AI – Comprehensive AI APIs for machine learning

Google Cloud AI offers a wide range of AI services that can be used via REST APIs or Python SDKs.

Main services:

- **Vertex AI** : End -to -end platform for ML models
- **Cloud Vision API** : Image recognition and object recognition
- **Cloud Natural Language API** : NLP for text analysis
- **Speech-to-Text & Text-to-Speech** : Speech recognition and synthesis
- **Translation API** : Automatic Translation

Areas of application:

- Image and text recognition for AI agents
- Analyzing Customer Feedback with NLP
- Automatic speech-to-text conversion for chatbots

32.3.2 AWS AI Services – Scalable AI solutions for enterprises

Amazon Web Services (AWS) offers a wide range of AI-powered cloud services that can be used for various applications.

Main services:

- **Amazon Rekognition** : Image recognition and facial analysis
- **Amazon Comprehend** : NLP and sentiment analysis
- **Amazon Lex** : Chatbot Development
- **Amazon Polly** : Text- to -Speech with natural language output
- **Amazon Forecast** : Time series analysis and forecast models

Areas of application:

- Facial recognition for security and access systems
- speech recognition for virtual assistants
- AI-powered financial forecasting with Amazon Forecast

32.3.3 Microsoft Azure AI – AI APIs for enterprises and cloud applications

Microsoft Azure AI provides powerful AI services that integrate well with Office 365 products and enterprise applications.

Main services:

- **Azure Cognitive Services** : Collection of AI APIs for vision, speech, search
- **Azure Machine Learning** : Platform for training your own ML models

- **Azure Bot Service** : Developing chatbots and virtual assistants
- **Azure Translator** : High-precision machine translation
- **Azure Form Recognizer** : Automatic extraction of data from documents

Areas of application:

- chatbots with natural language processing
- Automatic processing of invoices and forms
- translation and language assistants

32.3.4 OpenAI GPT – Advanced AI for Text Generation

OpenAI offers one of the most powerful language AI technologies with GPT (Generative Pre-trained Transformer).

Main services:

- **GPT-4** : Text generation for dialogue systems
- **DALL·E** : AI-supported image generation
- **Codex** : AI-assisted code creation

Areas of application:

- **Automated content creation**
- **AI-supported code generation**
- **Creation of chatbots with human-like communication**

32.4 Comparison of the most important AI cloud platforms

platform	Strengthen	areas of application
Google Cloud AI	Best NLP and Image Recognition APIs	Chatbots, image recognition, analytics
AWS AI Services	Scalable Cloud AI for Enterprises	speech processing, forecasting, cloud bots
Azure AI	Good integration with Office products	enterprise chatbots, document processing
OpenAI GPT	Best Text Generation	Automated texts, code generation

32.5 Conclusion

Cloud AI services enable developers to quickly and efficiently create powerful AI agents without having to train their own models.

- **Google Cloud AI and AWS AI** offer comprehensive services for NLP, image recognition and predictive models.
- **Azure AI** is ideal for **enterprise applications with cloud integration** .
- **OpenAI GPT** is suitable for **high-quality text and code generation** .

These platforms accelerate the development of scalable AI agents that can be used in chatbots, voice assistants, image recognition and predictive analytics.

Chapter 33: Current Trends in AI Agent Development

33.1 Introduction

The development of AI agents is in a rapid growth phase, driven by advances in deep learning, reinforcement learning, multimodal AI and autonomous systems. Modern agents are becoming more and more powerful and are taking on increasingly complex tasks in business, science and everyday life.

This chapter provides an overview of the most important current trends in AI agent development, including new technologies, innovative applications, and challenges for the future.

33.2 Multimodal AI agents: understanding text, images, speech and more

What is multimodal AI?

Multimodal AI agents can process different types of data simultaneously – such as text, images, videos, speech and sensor data. This improves their ability to solve complex tasks.

Application examples:

- **Google Gemini** : Can combine text, images and code to solve versatile tasks.
- **GPT-4V (Vision)** : Extends classic AI agents with image analysis functions.
- **Autonomous vehicles & robots** : Combine camera images, LIDAR sensors and word processing for better decision making.

Advantages:

- Agents understand and process complex contexts better.
- Improved interaction with users through multimodal input.
- More application possibilities in **medicine, industry and research** .

33.3 Generative AI for AI Agents: Automatic Content Creation and Communication

What is generative AI?

Generative AI (GenAI) uses large language models (LLMs) and deep learning to autonomously generate texts, images, code or music.

Current developments:

- **ChatGPT & Claude 3** : Human-like dialogue for customer service and support agents.
- **DALL·E & Stable Diffusion** : AI-generated images for visual agents.
- **Code Llama & GitHub Copilot** : Autonomous code generation for software development.

Areas of application for AI agents:

- Chatbots with natural language processing for support & advice.
- Automatic generation of content for marketing, social media & SEO.
- AI-supported software development through automated code creation.

Challenges:

- AI-generated content must be **checked for accuracy and ethics** .
- **Bias and misinformation** can occur unintentionally.
- High **computational effort** for training and operating large models.

33.4 Autonomous AI agents: independent planning and ability to act

What are autonomous agents?

Autonomous AI agents make their own decisions, set goals and perform tasks without direct human instruction.

Current technologies:

- **AutoGPT & BabyAGI** : AI agents that independently research and solve problems.
- **LangChain** : Allows AI agents to **access external databases and APIs** .
- **OpenAI Function Calling** : AI agents can **use web services independently** .

Areas of application:

- Automated research agents for knowledge management.
- Trading agents for financial markets and crypto trading.
- IT security agents that detect and combat cyber attacks.

Challenges:

- **Behavior that is difficult to predict** can lead to unexpected results.
- **Need for regulation** to avoid uncontrolled AI agents.
- **Data protection and security** when agents act independently on the web.

33.5 Reinforcement Learning: Learning through Reward in Real-World Applications

Current progress:

- **DeepMind AlphaZero** : Learned chess, Go and poker **without human training data**
.

- **Tesla FSD (Full Self- Driving)** : Uses **reinforcement learning** to improve driving strategies.

- **Google DeepMind & OpenAI Robotics** : Training robots with RL to **learn new tasks through trial and error** .

New fields of application:

- Autonomous drones for logistics and rescue operations.

- Optimization of production processes in industry.

- Game AI for intelligent NPCs (Non-Player Characters).

Challenges:

- RL requires **high computing power** and long training times.
- Simulations must be as realistic as possible to enable transfer to the real world.

33.6 AI agents for personal assistance & automation

Next-Gen Assistants:

Modern AI agents not only take on simple tasks, but can also automate complex processes.

Examples:

- **Google Assistant & Siri with LLM integration** : Voice assistants are becoming significantly more powerful.

- **Personal AI Agents (Pi by Inflection AI)** : Long-term interaction with users for **individual support** .

- **Notion AI & Microsoft Copilot** : **Automate office tasks** such as scheduling, document analysis, and project management.

Possible uses:

- Automatic appointment scheduling and calendar management.

- AI agents for personalized email and chat responses.

- Automatic code reviews and bug fixes for developers.

Challenges:

- **Privacy & security** are crucial for personalized AI agents.
- **Human control** must be maintained.

33.7 AI Safety and Ethics: Responsibility in the Development of Intelligent Agents

As the performance of AI agents increases, so does the responsibility to make them ethical and safe.

Critical topics:

- **AI bias & discrimination** : Agents could reinforce existing prejudices.

- **Deepfakes & Fake News** : Generative AI can create false information that is difficult to detect.

- **Autonomous decisions** : In the absence of human control, AI agents can perform unexpected actions.

Solutions:

- **Explainable AI (XAI):** Explainable decision making for trustworthy AI.
- **Regulations & AI laws:** The **EU AI Act** and other guidelines define clear rules.
- **Responsible AI & AI audits:** Companies implement **transparency and ethics guidelines** .

Example: OpenAI Alignment Research

- RLHF (Reinforcement Learning from Human Feedback) improves AI through human feedback.

- Security measures in GPT-4 to avoid inappropriate responses.

33.8 Conclusion

AI agent development is being revolutionized by multimodal models, generative AI, autonomous agents and reinforcement learning. While AI agents are becoming more and more powerful, security, ethics and transparency are critical challenges for the future.

The most important trends summarized:

- **Multimodal AI:** Agents understand text, speech, images and videos simultaneously.
- **Generative AI:** Automatic content creation and human-like dialogues.
- **Autonomous agents:** Independent problem solving without human commands.
- **Reinforcement Learning:** More Efficient Decision Making.
- **Personalized AI assistants:** automating everyday tasks.
- **Ethical AI:** Ensuring transparency and fairness.

The future of AI agents promises smarter, more flexible and more responsible systems that will have a lasting impact on our everyday lives and the economy.

Chapter 34: Future developments and visions for AI agents

34.1 Introduction

The rapid development of artificial intelligence (AI) has already led to revolutionary advances in AI agents. But what can we expect in the coming years? Visions of the future range from fully autonomous agents to hybrid human-AI interactions to intelligent networks of distributed AI systems.

34.2 Advances in multimodal and generalized AI agents

From specialized to generalized AI agents

Most current AI agents are specialized in specific tasks, such as chatbots, recommendation systems or game AI. The future belongs to more generalized agents that can flexibly adapt to different environments.

Future developments:

- **Multimodal AI** : AI agents are becoming even better at processing text, images, speech, videos and sensory data simultaneously.

- **Zero-shot and few -shot learning** : AI agents can learn new skills without extensive training, similar to humans.

- **Self-learning AI agents** : Agents can autonomously adapt their own learning processes in order to continuously improve.

Example:

- An AI agent for science could simultaneously analyze scientific texts, simulate experiments, and communicate with researchers to gain new insights faster.

34.3 Autonomous AI agents with true freedom of choice

From assistive to autonomous AI agents

While today's agents mostly work under human supervision, future AI agents could act largely autonomously – similar to human experts.

Possible areas of application:

- Autonomous financial agents that analyze markets and make investments independently.

- Medical AI agents that care for patients and make diagnoses.

- Self-managed smart cities in which AI agents optimize traffic flow, energy supply and public services.

Technological challenges:

- **Trustworthiness & Transparency** : How can autonomous agents make comprehensible decisions?
- **Legal framework** : What **regulations** are needed for independent AI agents?
- **Fault tolerance & safety** : How do we prevent unexpected behavior or errors in autonomous systems?

34.4 AI agents as part of the Internet of Things (IoT) and Smart Environments

AI agents as intelligent mediators in networked systems

In the future, AI agents could form the interface between people, machines and environments.

Future scenarios:

- **Smart Homes** : AI agents control lighting, heating and household appliances individually according to the needs of the residents.

- **Industrial automation** : Intelligent production plants could react independently to disruptions and optimize processes.

- **Autonomous supply chains** : AI agents coordinate the entire logistics from order to delivery in real time.

Advantages of this development:

- Higher efficiency through autonomous optimization.
- Lower resource consumption through data-driven control.
- Improved user experience through personalized interactions.

34.5 Human-AI interaction: Collaborative agents as co-pilots of everyday life

From AI as a tool to AI as a partner

Currently, AI agents are more like tools controlled by humans. However, the future could lie in true collaboration between humans and AI.

Possible developments:

- **AI co-pilots for work environments** : Intelligent assistants that support employees in real time.

- **AI-powered creativity** : Machines help designers, musicians and writers create **new works** .

- **Augmented Reality (AR) with AI** : Virtual AI agents help with complex tasks in Augmented Reality (AR), such as repairs or medical procedures.

Example:

- **AI in research** : AI agents could act as intelligent advisors, assisting scientists with hypotheses, data analysis and simulations.

34.6 Superintelligent AI agents: vision or danger?

What is artificial superintelligence (ASI)?

An artificial superintelligence (ASI) would be an AI that surpasses humans in almost all cognitive areas.

Theoretical possibilities:

- **Automated research & development** : AI agents could develop new technologies faster than humans.

- **Self-improving systems** : AIs could optimize themselves without human intervention.

- **Global problem solving** : Superintelligent systems could find solutions to climate change, disease and energy crises.

Challenges and risks:

- **Uncontrollability:** How can we ensure that a super AI acts in the interests of humanity?
- **Race for AI supremacy:** Geopolitical tensions could be exacerbated by unregulated AI development.
- **Ethics & Control:** Who decides on the goals and values of a superintelligent AI?

Solutions:

- Regulations & ethical guidelines for advanced AI agents.
- Safety mechanisms to prevent unpredictable behavior.
- Hybrid systems in which AI agents remain closely connected to human decision-making.

34.7 AI agents and the society of the future

How do AI agents change our lives in the long term?

With the increasing integration of AI agents into all areas of life, the question arises as to how society will deal with this transformation.

Long-term developments:

- **AI as an "everyday companion":** Constant interaction with intelligent systems that support personal and professional life.

- **Fully automated work processes:** Many jobs could be taken over or supported by AI agents.

- **New social structures:** Questions of labor distribution, ethics and regulation must be clarified.

Potential challenges:

- **Labor market changes:** What does a world look like in which many jobs are taken over by AI agents?
- **Data protection & privacy:** How do we protect personal data in an AI-driven society?
- **Cultural and philosophical questions:** What role should AI play in society in the long term?

34.8 Conclusion

The future development of AI agents will fundamentally change our world. Autonomous systems, multimodal agents, human-AI collaboration and superintelligence are just some of the key trends.

Summary of future visions:

- AI agents as intelligent companions in everyday life.
- Networked AI systems that are more efficient than today's technologies.
- Autonomous AI agents that control entire business processes.
- Superintelligence as a potential milestone or risk.

The coming years will show how AI agents could support, challenge or even transform humanity. Responsible AI development is key to making this future sustainable.

Chapter 35: Conclusion and Outlook

35.1 Introduction

The development of AI agents has made tremendous progress in recent years. From rule-based systems to machine learning to autonomous agents with multimodal capabilities, the technology is undergoing dynamic change.

This chapter summarizes the key findings of the book and provides an outlook on the future of AI agent development, looking at the most important achievements, open challenges, and potential developments for the coming years.

35.2 Summary of key findings

Basics of AI Agents

AI agents are autonomous or semi-autonomous systems that perform perception, decision-making and actions in an environment. They are divided into reactive, goal-oriented, utility-based and learning agents.

Technological advances

- **Deep learning and reinforcement learning** have accelerated the development of intelligent agents.

- **Multimodal models** enable AI agents to process different types of inputs (text, images, sound) simultaneously.

- **Generative AI** improves natural language processing and automation.

real-world applications

AI agents are used in **industry, medicine, finance, autonomous driving and smart homes**. They optimize processes, save costs and increase efficiency.

challenges and ethical issues

Despite the successes, challenges remain:

- **AI security and transparency** : Decisions made by AI agents must be traceable.
- **Ethical issues and bias** : AI must be designed fairly and without discrimination.
- **Regulations and legal framework** : The **EU AI Act** and other initiatives attempt to set clear guidelines.

35.3 Open challenges in AI agent development

1. Explainable and trustworthy AI

Current AI agents are often **black-box models** whose decisions are difficult to understand. **Explainable AI (XAI)** will be crucial to increasing trust in AI.

2. AI energy efficiency and sustainability

Training large AI models requires enormous computational resources. Future research should focus on **energy-efficient algorithms and green AI** .

3. Human-AI interaction

AI agents must be designed in such a way that they can be intuitively integrated into everyday human life. **Natural language processing, emotional intelligence and adaptive learning processes** are key research areas.

4. Security against misuse

As AI agents become more autonomous, the risk of **manipulation, cyberattacks and misconduct increases. Clear security mechanisms and regulations** are needed .

35.4 Visions for the future of AI agents

1. AI agents as everyday companions

- **Personalized digital assistants** that interact and learn with users over the long term.
- **AI coaches for health, education and finance** who provide personalized advice.

2. Fully autonomous agent systems

- **Autonomous delivery drones and vehicles** that operate without human intervention.
- **AI agents in science** that discover new drugs or theories.

3. Human-AI symbiosis

- **Brain-computer interfaces (BCI)** could enable a direct connection between humans and AI agents.
- **Augmented Reality (AR) with AI agents** that assist with tasks in real time.

4. Superintelligent AI

The idea of **artificial superintelligence (ASI)** remains a long-term vision – with opportunities and risks. Ethical and regulatory control will be essential.

35.5 Conclusion: Shaping the future with AI agents

AI agents will fundamentally change the way we work, communicate and live. Their potential is enormous - from increasing productivity in companies to personal assistants that make everyday life easier.

Important recommendations for action for the future:

- **Responsible AI development** : AI must be designed to be **safe, ethical and traceable**
  .
- **Interdisciplinary cooperation** : Research, industry and politics must jointly define AI standards.
- **Continuous training** : To work with AI, people must learn how to use it effectively.
- **Sustainable AI development** : Energy consumption and environmental impacts of AI should be minimized.

Final Outlook

AI agents are no longer a thing of the future, but a reality that already influences our everyday lives. The next few years will be crucial for how AI agents are developed, regulated and integrated into our lives.

The question is not whether AI agents will change our world – but how we actively shape this change.